JOHN GRUEN

People Who Dance

The New Bohemia
Close-up
The Private World of Leonard Bernstein
The Party's Over Now
The Private World of Ballet
Gian Carlo Menotti
Erik Bruhn: Danseur Noble
The World's Great Ballets

JOHN GRUEN

People Who Dance

22 Dancers Tell Their Own Stories

A DANCE HORIZONS BOOK

Princeton Book Company,
Publishers

A Dance Horizons Book
Princeton Book Company, Publishers
POB 57
Pennington, NJ 08534

ISBN 0-916622-74-6
LC # 88–60952

Editorial Supervisor: Richard Carlin
Cover and book design by Main Street Design
Typography by Delmas

Cover photograph of the Joffrey Ballet performing *Trinity,*
choreography by Gerald Arpino, by Herbert Migdoll

Copyright notice continues on page 177

CONTENTS

ACKNOWLEDGMENTS

My first thanks go to the dancers and choreographers represented in this book, who throughout the years have so generously shared their thoughts and feelings with me. For her care and diligence in the preparation of the manuscript, my special gratitude to Lise Friedman. For their unfailing support, I wish to thank Charles H. Woodford, President of Princeton Book Company, Publishers, and Richard Carlin, Editor and Marketing Director. My very special thanks to Richard Philp, Managing Editor of *Dance Magazine,* who originally edited most of the articles in this book. Finally, my deep-felt gratitude to my friend, William Como, Editor-in-Chief of *Dance Magazine,* who for nearly 15 years has given me the opportunity of writing for his publication, thus widening the scope of my knowledge and broadening my dance-writing experience. My tribute to Bill is that almost all of the interviews in *People Who Dance* were spearheaded by him and first appeared in different form in *Dance Magazine.*

Dancers are indeed people—people whose lives evolve within a circumscribed world yet are heir to the ongoing struggles and fleeting satisfactions common to us all. Unlike most of us, however, dancers strive for an ideal that is singularly unattainable: perfection. Their goal is to make visible an art that by definition requires utmost dedication and commitment, often at the expense of a fully realized personal life. The fact is, people who dance are willing slaves to a vision that places their art above all else. Their work, in whatever dance discipline, is predicated on the assumption that to dance is to live.

In gathering this material—selected interviews conducted over a period of some 15 years—I have come to realize that no matter how total their dedication, dancers, choreographers or company directors are nevertheless subject to the myriad vagaries of circumstance and fate—that their achievements have, for the most part, been attained at a price—that the realities of life have at times tragically intruded upon the course of brilliant careers.

But this is not a book of dance tragedies. On the contrary, it hopes to celebrate the lives of individuals who, from early childhood, have found deep and lasting fulfillment in a field that more than any other offers contact with the unparalleled joys of human movement, be it in the form of classical, modern, theater, or jazz dance.

Indeed, all the artists in this collection have in one way or another enriched our lives, and through their singular talent have made manifest the fact that dancers are not only people, but cherished and ineffable symbols of our better selves.

John Gruen
New York, 1988

For John Bass

Patrick Bissell

Patrick Bissell and Jolinda Menendez
Photograph by Max Waldman

Patrick Bissell

On May 11, 1978, at precisely 8:05 P.M., the curtain rose at the Metropolitan Opera on a performance of the "Kingdom of Shades" act of *La Bayadère,* presented by American Ballet Theatre (ABT) as part of a mixed bill during its 8-week spring season. The program listed Martine van Hamel in the role of Nikia and Patrick Bissell as Solor. One had come to love Miss van Hamel as the heroine of *La Bayadère;* she had danced the role on many previous occasions with exquisite and riveting effect. The unknown quantity of the evening would be Patrick Bissell, a 20-year-old dancer plucked from the corps and making his New York debut in a role usually danced by an experienced principal.

When the seemingly endless row of "Shades" completed its long, ethereal variation, the stage was suddenly ignited by the running, wind-swept figure of a tall young man in Oriental garb. It was a presence that announced the arrival of a dancer entirely in command of himself—a warrior prince ready to conquer not only his beloved Nikia, but also the more than 3000 people who had gathered at the Met. As the ballet progressed, it became clear that here was a young dancer of a very particular talent. The perfect symmetry of his line, the princely beauty of his face, the technical security and the proud mien of his carriage contrived to make one sit up and take note of the arrival of an exceptional young artist—a potential new star of the ballet stage.

Few people in the audience had ever heard of Patrick Bissell, but when the curtain fell on *La Bayadère,* they gave the boy a tumultuous ovation. And when, on the next morning, they opened their newspapers, Patrick Bissell was no longer an unknown quantity. Reviewers vied for adjectives to describe the dazzle and brilliance of his performance. In American show-biz tradition, an unknown had become an overnight sensation.

Some 10 days later, Bissell partnered Cynthia Gregory in yet another highly demanding work: Balanchine's *Theme and Variations.* Baryshnikov himself had been challenged by the speed and intricacies of this most difficult of male roles when he had danced it with Gelsey Kirkland only a few nights earlier. But once again, Patrick Bissell rose to the occasion, offering a surprising mastery in matters of control, clarity of line, and technical prowess. Moreover, his very special aristocratic bearing was the sort that 20-year-old corps dancers rarely evince. In the climactic pas de deaux, Bissell partnered Gregory with consummate attentiveness to the rarefied innuendos that can make partnerships come to life. In consort with a ballerina of acknowledged

1

greatness, this corps boy radiated a confidence and charm that transformed a pas de deaux into a personal encounter between two royal beings. A quality of regal maturity and dignity gave renewed credence to the fact that Patrick Bissell had indeed arrived.

One more performance, toward the end of the ABT season, gave evidence of Bissell's dramatic range. This was his portrayal of the role of Espada in Mikhail Baryshnikov's new production of *Don Quixote,* or *Kitri's Wedding.* Here was a toreador of magnetic dimension. Tall, lithe, and full of cocky self-appreciation, Bissell negotiated complex turns and split-second cape maneuvers with tongue-in-cheek wit and high good spirits. Again, there was authority, artistry, and a stage presence that brought cheers from the audience.

The head-spinning rise of any young dancer has its built-in dangers. The "too-much-too-soon" syndrome can backfire. Superlatives and accolades laid at the feet of a boy barely out of his teens can rob a rising youngster of objectivity. They can, in fact, damage his perception of what building a career is all about. However, Patrick Bissell came to his early prominence the hard way. His was not the smooth and disciplined road that other young dancers have traveled. For Bissell, the road was tortuous and fraught with difficult and humiliating setbacks. The genesis of his dancing career held little promise of a serious future. Headstrong, independent, quarrelsome, and all too often unmanageable, Bissell's personality and background could easily have led him into failure, despair, and serious trouble, as it often did. Perhaps only the inescapable need to dance helped him avoid the clutches of delinquency.

Bright and verbal to an alarming degree, Patrick Bissell's self-analysis in the following portrait offers the image of a young man struggling for his place in the sun. Erratically schooled, by turns stubborn and recondite, he managed his early life more through raw instinct than through intellect or common sense. In the end, his single-minded desire to dance—and to dance well—gave him the identity he yearned for.

In this interview conducted in 1978, Bissell gave his own version of his youth and first triumphs as a dancer. He was frank about his boyhood troubles—but glossed over many of the details of his life at home and school. I have added notes about some of the facts that have come to light about his life and times since 1978. I have also filled in information about his career to the time of his death in 1987. However, I feel strongly that these words stand as a memorial to a dancer who struggled against terrific personal and social odds to be one of the greatest ballet stars of our time.

Walter Patrick Bissell and William McDonald Bissell, fraternal twins, are born into the large Bissell family on December 1, 1957, in Corpus Christi, Texas. A life of almost continuous and disruptive travel is in store for the twins, their older brother, and two sisters.

"My father is a computer engineer, and the work he was involved in caused him to move constantly from state to state. So, we lived in Corpus Christi for 3 or 4 months, then we moved to California. At one point, we lived in Chicago, then we moved back to California, then we lived in five different cities in Ohio. Actually, I spent most of my time growing up in the state of Ohio. My mother is essentially a theater person—not professionally, but she performed in local playhouse groups ... just to keep her going. But, of course, she had a family to rear.

"About my twin brother: he's fraternal, not identical. Everything I am, he is not. In a way that's good, because it makes you grow up on your own. There's no competition. His name is Bill. My nickname is Wally. Bill's interest is religion. He has been to ministry school in St. Louis, but he wasn't very pleased with it. However, he's done a lot of preaching, and he's helped alcoholics. My parents have always tried to influence us in matters of religion. For me, it didn't work. I never wanted to go to church and never really believed in it. We'd have awful fights on Sunday mornings about my going to church! I just couldn't stand the idea of going. My brother, on the other hand, always went. He's not a fanatic and he doesn't push religion on people. But then, he's not a pushy person. He's the calmest, most laid-back, and relaxed person imaginable. I feel that anyone who is as compassionate, patient, and good as Bill deserves the best that life can offer. But I think he's always going to be a loner.*

"I have an older brother. His name is Donald Bissell, which is also my father's name. Don is a big one. He's about 6 foot 7 inches. He's gone to college and has been involved in sports. We were very close, the closest in the family. We had common interests, not the dance, but things we did in our spare time. Through Don, I got interested in sports. I played baseball, football, basketball, ran track ... I did it all.

"There's my sister Barbara. She attended Berkeley and majored in French which she speaks fluently. Ultimately, she wants to go to Paris and study mime with Marcel Marceau. She and I are the only ones actively involved in theater. When we were younger, we fought

*William Bissell now works in manufacturing.

3

like cats and dogs. When there are five kids, there are always two who have to fight. Well, Barbara and I fought.

"The oldest in my family is my sister Susan. She's the one who got me involved in dancing. She had studied dancing, but never became a professional. Instead, she's become a sailmaker and lives in San Francisco. She makes sails for boats and is very much involved with the sea. It's wonderful for her, because she leads a very healthy life, and she's happy. A few years ago she married a "boat-y," a guy who lives on boats. On the West Coast, there's a whole society of people who live on boats in marinas. They're little towns within themselves. Anyways, Susan's husband could never keep a steady job, and my sister found that a hard way to live. So, they divorced."*

Patrick Bissell begins his dance training at the age of 10 in Toledo, Ohio. It is his sister Susan who urges him to study with her own dancing teacher. "A young boy like you would inspire him so much!" she tells her young brother.

"The teacher's name was Bud Kerwin. He was a wonderful, wonderful man and a wonderful teacher. He's now teaching at Butler University in Indianapolis. When I went to him, he had a small ballet school. There'd be four or five of us in a class, and we got a lot of attention. He inspired you to be a prince. He'd say, 'Stick out your chest and think of yourself wearing a beautiful velvet jacket covered with fabulous jewels, emeralds, diamonds, and rubies!' He'd set all these visions in your brain! And he made you feel you were really something. The steps he gave you were primitive, but you were dancing! He really pulled that out of you.

"At the time, we lived in a pretty rich neighborhood, and I was going to grade school. The kids I went to school with were more educated in the arts, and it didn't matter that I was taking ballet lessons. I didn't get into any hassles. In fact, I entered some local talent shows, and while I didn't win any prizes, people thought that was really nice.

"But then, we moved to a farming town called Swenton, outside of Toledo. Well, that was different. The kids there had fun doing things I never heard of before—stupid, horrible things like torturing cats. I

---

*It is interesting to note that in his portrait of his family, Patrick omitted only his mother. His relationship with her was a stormy one. His mother suffered from bouts of severe depression and anger and eventually became addicted to the prescription tranquilizer Milltown. Patrick struggled throughout his childhood to gain her love, a love that came only in fits and starts. Bissell's mother admitted in a recent interview that she physically abused the child despite the fact that she loved him.

ended up getting into a lot of trouble in Swenton. In fact, that's where things really began to sour for me, because we ended up living in that farm town for three years. I tried to keep my dancing lessons a secret for as long as possible, but when the kids found out about it, it was hell. I was in fights every single day for two years. I was continually being called a sissy and was never left alone about it. It was horrible. Of course, I didn't learn a thing at school. I was almost 13-years-old, and with all the flack I was getting from the other kids, I just never stopped being in trouble at school. Despite it all, I continued my ballet classes with Bud Kerwin and stayed with him for 2 years. Then, when Mr. Kerwin left for Indianapolis, I quit going. And, anyway, at around that time my father got another job and we all moved to Granville, Ohio."

Patrick Bissell enters high school in Granville, Ohio. His father asks him, "What are you going to do when you grow up?" Patrick says, "I'm going to be a dancer!" Patrick alone is elated over the prospect.

"My dad didn't think that being a dancer was sissy or anything like that. He just thought it wouldn't be a good way of making a living. He didn't know that dancers could have a splendid life and earn lots of money. Well, you know, Dad is very American in that way—he thinks in terms of money and retirement and all that kind of garbage that I don't really believe in. Anyway, when we moved to Granville, I started going to high school and also found a new teacher in Columbus. She was a Russian lady named Tatjiana (Tania) Smith. The reason she was called Smith was that she married an American by that name. She was a wonderful teacher, and being Russian, she really inspired us. There were some very good dancers in her classes; I began to work very hard and to improve a lot.

"But then there was the business of regular school. The high school I went to was horrendous. I didn't make friends there, and people didn't like me very much. All my friends were at the ballet class, and at school I was again being razzed and made fun of. I was still a scrawny kid, and there were kids there who could crush me in a minute. Well, my school work just went downhill. I mean, I'd go to school, then take a bus into Columbus, take ballet class, have rehears-als for small performances we gave, and by the time I got back to Granville it was midnight. The last thing I felt like doing was my home-work. It was a mess. I was making Ds and Fs and Cs. I would get thrown out of class. I'd always be sent to the principal's office. It was awful, and I was getting a terrible reputation.* Even though I was just a kid, I could never stand people telling me how to live my life. I couldn't stand people telling me what to do and how to behave. If I couldn't work things out my way, I was unhappy. That's the way I was. Anyway, I got to be known as a big troublemaker, and I just couldn't stand it anymore. I had to get out of Granville. I also felt I had gotten as much out of Tania Smith as I could. I had worked with her for a year-and-a-half and felt it was time to move on. Basically, I had to get away from everything. I never graduated from high school, and I couldn't have cared less."

In 1972, at the age of 15, Patrick Bissell applies for and receives a scholarship at The National Academy of the Arts in Champaign, Illinois.

"At the time I went there, the place was called The National Academy of Dance. It had wonderful teachers: Lupe Serrano, Michael Maule, Stella Applebaum, and Anthony Valdor. This was a new school, and they were handing out tons of scholarships. They had academics and a work program—it was great. The Academy was run by Dr. Gilbert Wright, and he had very high moral standards. But he was a nice guy and had worked wonders with the school. Well, things worked out for me for about a year there. We had two 2-hour technique classes every day, and that was very hard, especially at my age. But I loved the classes, and I got to be popular with the other students. I really worked hard for about a year, but then, I got into trouble again. You see, for the first time in my life I was on my own, and I guess I felt like letting loose. I couldn't wait to get out of class and go out and socialize and have fun. I had a girl friend and I stayed up late. I'd be tired and groggy when I woke up mornings. Then there was the matter of my academics, which you had to take along with the dance classes. I had trouble keeping up with the other students, and the whole mess started up again. I didn't really know *what* I wanted at that point, although I never once thought I was going to stop dancing. But I had this tremendous urge to be on my own and be a dancer and earn my own living and get my own apartment . . . but I was only 15! So, it ended up that I was going to lose my scholarship because I had lost my direction and couldn't keep up with my studies.

"I'd blown it again! I really screwed myself up this time! The upshot was that the administration decided to send me back home.

*It was at this time that Bissell began drinking, using drugs, and committing small burglaries. This behavior exacerbated his troubles in school and at home.

Michael Maule was relegated to take me to the bus station.* He bought my ticket back to Granville and ... what was I going to do there? I was so angry! I was so upset! Michael Maule kept telling me, 'Whatever happens, you mustn't stop dancing!' He was upset too. He told me, 'I'm sorry this happened. But we warned you. We told you to shape up!' Well, he was perfectly right in sending me away. I really *did* louse things up for myself. But, my God! I *didn't* want to go back to Granville.

"So, the bus came in. I had my bus ticket and maybe two or three dollars in my pocket. Michael made sure I got on the bus and then left. Well, I just couldn't face going back home. So, what I did as sit in the bus for about two blocks, and then I got up and rushed to the bus driver, saying: 'Oh, my God! I left something at the bus station and I have to get off! Could you please give me my ticket back and write something on it so I can get a refund and catch a later bus!' Well, the bus driver stopped the bus and let me off. He returned my ticket and I ran back to the bus station, cashed in the ticket, and somehow found a big piece of cardboard on which I wrote a sign saying 'SAN FRAN-CISCO.' I stood on the highway, holding up the sign because I was going to hitchhike to San Francisco and see my sister Susan. She was the only person I felt I could turn to. I waited and waited, I was shaking and on the verge of crying. Finally, somebody picked me up, and I was off!

"From that moment on, I felt free. It felt so good to be free! I had $20.00 in my pocket from the ticket I had cashed in, and I ended up arriving in San Francisco having spent only $3.00 of it. People treated me well, and I had some pretty interesting experiences hitchhiking all that way. Truck drivers would pick me up so I would talk to them and keep them awake. I remember one time being dropped off in the middle of nowhere in Oklahoma. It was 2:00 A.M., and I slept by the side of the road. Actually, I thought it was all very adventurous and I loved it.

"Finally, I got to San Francisco and called my sister who, at the time, was living with her husband on a boat. When I got to the boat I called my father, who was very worried because he had expected me home. When I talked to him and explained how I felt, he was angry. But I could tell he was also kind of proud of me. He was trying to scold me and to be firm and act like a father, but I sensed he was proud. I was kind of proud, too, because I was still only 15 and had crossed practically the whole damned country on my own."

---

*Maule recently disclosed that Bissell was expelled for selling marijuana to other students.

Patrick Bissell, desperate to find a dancing job, auditions for the San Francisco Ballet. He is promptly turned down, but Harold Christensen, head of the San Francisco Ballet School, offers him a partial scholarship that includes a small stipend for living expenses. Barely able to live, and unhappy at the school, young Bissell decides to return home to Granville, Ohio.

"Everything would have been all right if I had been accepted into the San Francisco Ballet, but they didn't take me. I stayed at the school for a couple of months, but I felt like a lost soul there. Besides, I was living on the boat with my sister and her husband, and it was pretty tight. It just didn't work out. Finally, I made up my mind to hitchhike back to Granville. I even thought of finishing high school. Well, when I got back, my parents said they'd like to enroll me at the North Carolina School of the Arts, but, of course, I'd have to audition in order to get in. I was pretty much out of shape, so I took some classes at a local ballet school, just to get my stamina back. After some weeks, it was time to go and audition in North Carolina.

"My parents put me on a bus at 7:00 P.M., and I got there at three in the morning. My audition was scheduled for 10:00 A.M. the same morning. I was completely exhausted. Of course, the school was closed when I arrived, and I tried to get a few hours sleep on a bench on the school grounds. At 7:00 A.M. the Student Commons opened up, and I went there to get a cup of coffee. I tried to keep myself awake. At 10:00 that morning, I took the audition. Well, I was a nervous wreck! All the teachers sat at this long table. I did the best I could and didn't feel too badly about the audition. When it was over, they called me up front. One of the teachers was Robert Lindgren. He told me that the school had heard from Michael Maule, and he had said that I was talented. But they had also heard about my past history in Champaign, Illinois. Mr. Lindgren said that they'd like to take me, but that I would have to really shape up. In fact, they only took me on for the summer session— and only on probation.

"So, I went back home to wait for the summer session to begin. My parents were excited for me, but they were also worried about my being able to stick it out. They said, 'O.K., this is your last chance. Do good this time!' Well, at this point I was really wanting to do good. I was tired of screwing up and making things bad for myself. I was really ready to go gung-ho and do things right.*

---

*During this summer at home, Patrick's mother attempted to commit suicide by taking an overdose of tranquilizers. Patrick discovered her and helped his father drag her to the hospital.

"When I got to North Carolina, I straightened up and went to all my classes and for the first time *really* worked hard as a dancer. The teachers there were terrific: Duncan Noble, Gina Vidal, Noland Dingman. They took me from being a student to being close to a professional dancer. After 1 year, I danced the lead in the *Nutcracker,* which for that place was the big deal. They also had a company called the North Carolina Dance Theater, and I had danced a concert with them for the opening of the Agnes de Mille Theatre. They worked me hard. I was dancing so much that I really didn't have time left over for my academics. There was no time for homework—and there was a lot of it there. And, again, that was my downfall.

"I was very run-down and tired and started to feel itchy again. Towards the end of the year, things started getting very tense. Two weeks before the end of the school year, I had accumulated so many violations that they finally threw me out of the school. They had an appeals committee, and I could have appealed, but I wasn't going to. I just had had it and I was leaving."*

While still at the North Carolina School of the Arts, Patrick Bissell is offered a 6-week Ford Foundation Scholarship to the School of American Ballet (SAB). The scholarship is offered to him by Violette Verdy who is scouting for dance students. At the age of 16, Bissell travels to New York, confident that after his 6 weeks at Balanchine's school, he'd be asked back.

"I left the North Carolina School of the Arts on pretty bad terms, which was too bad, because I really liked that school and feel that it was responsible for giving me a lot of good training. Anyway, the School of American Ballet was a wonderful experience. In addition to the 6 weeks, they paid me $200.00 a month, which of course wasn't enough to live on. I called my parents about getting more money, but they were very angry and said they wouldn't support me unless I went back to regular school. Well, I had no intention of doing that, so I decided to start auditioning for some companies near New York. I auditioned for the Boston Ballet and for the Pennsylvania Ballet. In Boston, the audition went well, but, unfortunately, E. Virginia Williams, the head of the company, wasn't there when I auditioned. James Capp gave the class, and he told me that I should come back because he was sure Miss Williams would take me. I said I'd think about it. Then I auditioned for the Pennsylvania Ballet, and they offered me a 2-week summer session on scholarship. So, after the SAB session, I did that and, boy,

*Again, drug problems plagued the young dancer.

9

did they work us there! It was a real workout—5 or 6 hours a day of your modern, your character, your adagio, your 2-hour technique with Ben Harkarvy. It was hard! And I found that Mr. Harkarvy was a hard man to please. But I felt that Barbara Weissberger, who heads the company, really liked me. Well, at the end of the session, she offered me an apprenticeship and $60.00 a week. I thought about it for a while and then decided to go back to Boston and audition again for Virginia Williams. When Miss Williams saw me, she said, 'Sign this boy up!' I was given a year's contract."

At 17, Patrick Bissell enters the corps of the Boston ballet. He improves rapidly and is quickly given solo parts in *Nutcracker*, *Sleeping Beauty*, and *Carmina Burana*.

"It was excellent training, of course, and I worked like mad trying to learn aerial tricks and to really improve my ballet technique. The trouble in Boston was that one didn't get to perform very often. They had weekend seasons, and all we'd do was rehearse and rehearse for only four or five performances. I also felt there wasn't much inspiration in the management there. But I figured that if I were employed for a year, I could then quit and collect unemployment. And that's what I finally did. I came back to New York, collected unemployment, went straight back to the School of American Ballet, and worked mainly with Stanley Williams. I was now 18 and began to be concerned about my image. I cut my hair and carried myself in a more mannerly fashion. Well, right away Stanley Williams started working with me, which I didn't expect at all. He really paid a lot of attention to me, which was great. Then, one day, Lincoln Kirstein peered into the class. He looked strange and imposing and I thought, 'Well, he must be somebody important.' I didn't really know who he was. But he kept coming back and looking at me. At one point, he pulled me out of class and told me, 'I think you're promising. I think you'll do well here. I'm going to talk to Rosemary Dunleavy and see if we can put you in company class and see what Mr. Balanchine thinks.' I thought, 'Oh, my God!' I just couldn't believe it.

"A few days later, I took company class and sensed that something was wrong. I talked to some people at the school, and they thought it was wrong for me to take company class. Some of the teachers said I shouldn't be doing that. There was flack about it. People were getting jealous. Well, I went to Lincoln Kirstein, who had told me to do this, and he told me not to listen to anybody—just to continue taking company class. Then, strangely enough, Mr. Kirstein came to me and said that I *should stop* taking company class but continue taking regular classes. So, that's what I did. And things went well.

"At one point I had a lot of people telling me that I should audition for American Ballet Theatre. They thought it was the right company for me. To tell you the truth, I didn't really understand the New York City Ballet all that much. I didn't understand Mr. Balanchine or the concept behind his ballets, most of which I hadn't seen. I hadn't been thinking about things like style, because I was concentrating so hard on class and on getting a strong technique. I was into getting eight pirouettes down pat. Anyway, I continued working with Stanley Williams and felt I was improving immensely. Naturally, I was also hoping to be taken in the City Ballet, whether I understood it or not.

"All the while, Stanley helped me incredibly. He made me aware of music, of phrasing, of how to dance things *within* the music, and of how much music *was* dance. But at 18, you're just like an athlete. You've got all this energy you want to let loose; I just tried to jump as high as I could. But Stanley called me down on that and let me think about rotation of legs and muscles. He wasn't into pyrotechnics. Then I got working with André Kramerevsky; he had that Russian thing and was fantastic about teaching all the tricks.

"I felt that the City Ballet needed boys, and I had really improved. But I didn't hear anything from the company. I mean, I was tall and felt I was just right for the company. I had filled out and looked more like a young man than just a boy. I really began looking at the City Ballet dancers. I looked at Peter Martins and he became an idol. I tried to imitate him and just by watching him I *did,* finally, understand the Balanchine style. I was getting hooked. I felt that the New York City Ballet was where I wanted to be. And I was overwhelmed by Mr. B.'s personality. He was like an emperor. I respected him enormously because he really changed the way Americans dance. The fact is, I was dying to dance in his ballets.

"Unfortunately, I felt that Mr. B. wasn't really interested in me. I felt he didn't like me. I think he thought that I was only interested in jumping and turning and doing tricks. And, of course, that's not what he's about. I think he *knew* I wanted to do those things and that I wasn't ready for him.

"But I continued working. I got the opportunity to work with Jerome Robbins. I learned the Green Boy part in his *Dances at a Gathering,* and I just loved it. Jerry would work with you, and he didn't so much care what you were doing as long as you got the feeling behind the steps. He wanted you to create a mood. Well, it was fantastic dancing that role, and I think Jerry liked me. Of course, mastering Mr. Balanchine's works was another matter. It would mean going back to the beginning. But I was ready. I was hoping and hoping he'd take me into the company—but it didn't happen. He took Paul Boos instead. Now, Paul had been there for a very long time, and he deserved to be taken into the company. Still, I was jealous. I wanted to be taken in. I needed to be taken in. I was upset and angry.

"One day I heard that Lucia Chase had called Stanley Williams and said, 'I need some boys.' She gets lots of her boys from Stanley. So he sent me over to American Ballet Theatre (ABT). Well, I thought that ABT was so star-studded that I'd never get anywhere there. I mean, they had Baryshnikov and Bujones and Clark Tippet and Charles Ward—people who were really good. But I was ready to get into a big company, so I took the audition."

In May, 1977, at the age of 19, Patrick Bissell is faced with a dilemma. The years of turmoil, setbacks, and hard work have begun to pay off. Suddenly, he is in greater demand than he had bargained for.

"The audition for Lucia Chase at ABT went well. Lucia said that they had four apprentice contracts and one corps contract. I told her I wasn't interested in any apprenticeship. She agreed to take me into the corps and offered me a 6-week try-out contract. For some reason, I felt I had to go and speak personally to Mr. Balanchine. I was very nervous, but I wanted to let him know that I really wanted to dance for him, but that I needed a job. I told him about my ABT contract. I told him that I was going to do the 6 weeks at ABT, but what I *really* wanted to do was to dance with the City Ballet. I really didn't want to go to ABT at this point. Well, he was very nice and told me to go to ABT and, after 6 weeks there, he'd see what he could do.

"Then, things got really crazy. Just before I started at ABT, Mr. Balanchine asked me to join the New York City Ballet! I had a contract from both companies! I became incredibly confused. I thought: '*What am I going to do?*' I talked to Stanley Williams and he said: 'You'll just have to make up your own mind.' He added that wherever I went, I couldn't lose. He felt I would do well at either place. Well, I listened to what everybody said and ultimately decided to join American Ballet Theatre.

"I figured that if I joined the City Ballet, I'd be put in the back row of the corps, and Mr. B. would just let me wait which is what he does—and which is good. But I had all this energy I wanted to let loose and I *did* want to dance the bravura things. And so, I joined ABT. I gave myself 3 years in the corps. If by that time I weren't given soloist things, I'd leave. So, there I was in the corps, not really doing very much. Then, the company went on its European tour—that was the summer of 1977—and they left me behind. Still, I knew I had a contract and would be dancing with them in New York, and at the Met.

"I worked hard in class—worked my rear end off—and the person who really nurtured me at ABT was Jürgen Schneider. He just worked me to death, and it really paid off. I didn't really dance all that much during the first Met season. Then, we went on a long cross-country tour, and when we landed in Washington, DC, I got word that I would be learning the role of Solor in *La Bayadère*. It just knocked me off my feet! I couldn't believe it! I mean, I hadn't done anything—anything that was hard. Then, all of a sudden, *La Bayadère*! It's really the most technically demanding thing you can do. I thought, 'Why did they decide to use *me*?' Well, it was a matter of good timing. Chuck Ward had just left the company, and Clark Tippet was having knee problems. Because he was working so much all of the time they needed a tall boy to learn *La Bayadère*. So, Lucia Chase came to me and said that she and the ballet masters had decided to give me this chance. Boy! Was my adrenalin going! I couldn't sleep at night. I was *so* looking forward to it. Jürgen Schneider was the one who told Lucia I was ready to do this, and he worked on it with me. I thank him a million times for helping me like this, because if he hadn't given me the attention, none of this would have happened."

In January, 1978, at the age of 20, Patrick Bissell begins to hit his stride in major roles. The irresponsible, brash kid of former years blossoms into a professional and distinguished young dancer. He learns the meaning of responsibility and lives up to his promise.

"I did my first *La Bayadère* in Los Angeles with Martine van Hamel. And she was just a charm, just a grace. I couldn't think of a better person to work with on my first performance. She made me feel calm— and she was *so* beautiful in the ballet. I felt I had to do my best, because I was dancing with such a world-famous ballerina. Well, it was hell, but I got through it. It totally drained me, but I didn't fall over. The company began to have faith in me. I did another *La Bayadère* with Jolinda Menendez, and it went well. When I did it with Jolinda, it was the first time I felt relaxed. Then, suddenly, Clark Tippet injured himself. And *Nutcracker* was coming up. He was to have danced it with Leslie Browne in Chicago. Instead, I got to do it. Misha Baryshnikov helped me with it, and he made me feel good about it. It was my very first full-length ballet, and I got through it. Then Misha said I'd be doing it at the Met. I was so happy! I was getting stronger. My stamina was building. I was gaining confidence.

"Then came the Met season in New York in Spring 1978. I got word that I would do *Theme and Variations*—my first Balanchine ballet! I was supposed to have danced it with Martine, but she was out injured. I was told I'd do it with Cynthia Gregory. Well, I've respected Cynthia forever. She's one of the first ballerinas I ever saw. I think she's just gorgeous. As a young man I had real fantasies about dancing with Cynthia. To think that it was coming true—that I was actually going to be dancing with Cynthia Gregory—was just so unreal to me! Well, what can I say? It was just overwhelming working with her. I wanted to do my very best so that she would like me, so that we would work more together. And then, we did it. We did *Theme!* I went to Stanley Williams who helped me with the double pirouettes to *à la seconde* and with the *rond de jambes en l'air.* They're hard, but I felt very natural doing them. It felt effortless to partner Cynthia. I mean, she didn't need to have me there, she can do it all on her own. I was there just to make sure she was on her leg here and there. Everybody told me how grueling the pas de deux was. But I didn't find it grueling. I just lifted her a couple of times, and the rest of it was there. Of course, I was nervous because I was so respectful of Cynthia. I wanted to do everything just right."

Patrick Bissell assesses his future and speaks of his newfound celebrity.

"Well, it's all very new to me. I'm still a young dancer, and I feel I have a long way to go. I've got a *lot* to learn about dancing, so I want people to just stick with me and allow me to grow. I want to have a long and lasting career in which I can develop into an artist. I really want to dance well. I don't want to go out there and dance spectacles—do a few tricks, be flamboyant, and get the public to like me. I want to fulfill myself and develop as an artist. To be a star ... well, some people think, 'Boy! Wouldn't that be great!' But I don't feel that way about it. It's nice to have the attention, but all I'm really interested in is to grow and to develop and to become an artist."

On December 29, 1987, Patrick Bissell was found dead in his apartment in Hoboken, NJ, by Amy Rose, a young ABT dancer with whom he was romantically involved. He was 30 years old. Autopsy results reveal that his death was caused by an overdose of cocaine, codeine, methadone, and other drugs.

Clearly, the remarkable self-command and brio that Bissell demonstrated onstage first in the corps de ballet, then as soloist, and finally as principal dancer, masked an offstage life plagued by tremendous self-doubt, insecurity, and depression. His good luck in landing challenging roles with leading dancers and choreographers continued through 1978 and 1979. He was invited by Natalia Makarova to be her partner in a new work with the Hamburg Ballet, and on his return to New York, he was given half a dozen new roles. Antony Tudor choreographed *The Tiller in the Fields* for Bissell and Gelsey Kirkland. Bissell's boundless energy—often fueled by alcohol and drugs—enabled him for a time to tackle an endless variety of roles with barely any rehearsal. Soon, however, the drinking and drug taking would take a toll on his performances.

In the early 1980s, the drug and alcohol abuse that he had for the better part of his youth managed to keep only "semi-public" began to encroach on his professional life. Due to his increasingly erratic behavior in rehearsal and performance, ABT fired—and rehired—him in 1980 and 1981 along with Gelsey Kirkland, who recently wrote about their mutual cocaine addiction in her autobiography *Dancing on My Grave.*

Bissells' relationship with Kirkland began with a frantic night of cocaine use. He dropped his previous relationship with Jolinda Menendez, an ABT ballerina who had had a somewhat stabilizing effect upon his life. After being fired from ABT, Bissell and Kirkland embarked on a tour that was marked by failures to show up or failures to perform to standard. The critics lambasted the pair, while their love changed quickly to mutual distrust and animosity.

By summer 1981, Bissell's career had lapsed in a tailspin. The low point was reached when the dancer tried to commit suicide. He was obviously calling out for help. In the fall, he managed to reconcile himself with Menendez and swore off his period of debauchery with Kirkland. He toured Latin America in Spring of 1982 and that June married Menendez.

Sadly, though, this marriage was short-lived, and Patrick's troubles with drugs continued. In 1985, ABT made his employment contract contingent upon his taking counseling and therapy for drug use and, in the fall of 1987, sent him for a 5-week stay for drug and alcohol abuse at the Betty Ford Clinic in Palm Springs, California. Ironically, after the program, Bissell appeared in better shape than he had been for years, and many people at ABT believed he would be dancing in the Spring 1988 season. No one suspected that he was using drugs again.

Bissell's tragic and untimely death has reopened the whole question of substance abuse within the dance community as a whole, first addressed in Kirkland's book *Dancing on My Grave.* Obviously, today's superstar dancers face many temptations. Bissell's life story—one of physical abuse, neglect, delinquency, and an endless need for love—made him a prime candidate for these problems. As he told me in 1978, "Thinking back on it all, I really think I've been incredibly lucky. I mean, it could have gone another way for me. The fact is, if I weren't a dancer, I would have been teenage hoodlum!"

Photograph by Jack Vartoogian

Alessandra Ferri

It would seem that Alessandra Ferri has done little wrong in the 8 short years of her dancing career. Luck and opportunity have consistently been part of her rise, and she has been quick to meet every challenge. As a full-page magazine ad for Scotch has been proclaiming for months, Ferri is "focused, passionate and strong-minded. At 97 pounds, she's nobody's weakling." More to the point, her temperament—theatrical and impulsive—has given the ballet stage an altogether new and salutary vision of dance.

An overnight sensation in London's Royal Ballet, Ferri became the favorite of choreographer Kenneth MacMillan, who entrusted her with leading roles in his *Mayerling, Manon,* and *Romeo and Juliet.* While somewhat unformed technically and not yet strong enough to assume roles in the major classics, her performances in MacMillan's full-length ballets were infused with such passion and musicality, such dramatic intensity and emotional clarity, that audiences took this teenage dancer fully to their hearts. Indeed, there was no question that Ferri—the first foreign-born dancer to be invited to join the Royal Ballet—had arrived.

But where did Ferri spring from?

"I was born on May 6, 1963, in Milan, Italy," she replies. "My father is an engineer. My mother is just my mother. I have a brother, 6 years older, who is in sports. My family members are my happiness. They are what keep me on the ground. I'm very close to them. They're very real people. Very honest. Very supportive. I went to a Catholic school where they gave ballet classes once a week. I started taking them when I turned 6. Then, at age 10, I entered the La Scala Opera Ballet School. Of course, Carla Fracci was our big inspiration; she was the great ballet diva of Italy and of the world. At La Scala, I worked with a very good teacher—Ljuba Dobrievich. She was of the Russian school, but had spent many years with (Maurice) Béjart. She gave us a whole new idea about dance, making us realize that dancing was theater—that you could really take things much further—give life to everything you did. She was inspiring.

"Unfortunately, after 3 years, Ljuba left La Scala to follow her husband, an opera director. By this time, I was 14, and I began to realize that life at La Scala would be very difficult. The teachers there really weren't very good, and the rules of the ballet company were impossibly strict. I mean, they had rule that once you joined the company, you had to wait 15 years before you could be given principal parts. I immediately understood there wasn't much future for me there. I had to make a decision: either I'd go elsewhere for further study of I'd just give up dancing."

It was Ferri's teacher, Ljuba Dobrievich, then residing in Florence, who strongly advised the 15-year-old to keep on dancing—it would be her life, she insisted. Dobrievich quickly arranged an audition at the Royal Ballet School in London. Ferri was instantly accepted. The year was 1978, and London would be Ferri's home for the next 6 years.

"I was incredibly happy in London. I was so excited to find what I wanted—I was ecstatic. I had great teachers, especially Julia Farron who made me understand the kind of dancer I was. You see, I started out having a kind of false notion about my dancing. I confused strong personality with strong dancing. Miss Farron made me look inside myself. She made me realize that you didn't have to be a big butch dancer to come across, that my strength would show without having to push it. So that was great. Well, at one point, I entered the Lausanne Competition and won one of the three prizes. Then, the British Council offered me a scholarship to continue my studies at the Royal Ballet School which meant my parents didn't have to continue supporting me. I worked for another year and then was taken into the company. They had a rule that only British subjects could join the company, but they changed this ruling, and I was the first foreign-born member. I joined in 1980."

It was Norman Morrice, then director of the Royal Ballet, who invited Ferri into the company. He and Kenneth MacMillan had seen Ferri in a school performance of MacMillan's *Concerto* and were notably impressed. Ironically, Ferri's Royal Ballet debut was not in a MacMillan ballet, but in the work of an American: Jerome Robbin's *Afternoon of a Faun.* She next danced the Gypsy Girl in Frederick Ashton's *The Two Pigeons,* after which came the starring role in MacMillan's *Mayerling,* which brought her extraordinary success. In Alessandra Ferri, as in Lynn Seymour, MacMillan had found a new muse, and with her, a new surge of creativity.

Important roles were fashioned on Ferri, notably in *L'Invitation au Voyage, Valley of Shadows, Isadora, Consort Lessons, Different Drummer,* and *Chanson.* For her performance in *Valley of Shadows,* a ballet based on the novel *The Garden of the Finzi-Contini,* Ferri won the prestigious Laurence Olivier Award. The Royal Ballet's artistic reputation was revitalized by a young Italian ballerina whose every performance seemed to promise new and ever widening wonders. It was also clear that Ferri was being molded into a MacMillan dancer, a fact that eventually proved problematic.

"It all started in 1983," Ferri remembers. "People and the critics all said that I was fine as a MacMillan dancer, but that I wasn't really a classical ballerina. Also, after my first performance in Kenneth's *Romeo and Juliet,* I received my first really bad review. I went into shock. I mean, most of the reviews were really quite good, but this *one* review was just horrible. It said I didn't understand anything, and that I was all wrong. Well, it went right into me, and I was really hurt, because I was 19 at the time, and I wanted *everybody* to love me. But it was also a life lesson. It made me realize that you can't be loved by everybody in the world, and also, that you don't perform to impress—only because you really love what you dance.

"Anyway, I swallowed all that. But something else was gnawing at me, and it was that the Royal wasn't giving me any of the classical roles—the *Giselles,* the *Swan Lakes,* the *Sleeping Beauties.* I just couldn't understand it. Finally, I went to management and asked, 'Why no classical roles for me?' They said I was not ready for them, that I didn't have the technique. Well, it's true. I *didn't* have the technique, but after all, I was a principal dancer, and I could *learn.* All I needed was the opportunity to dance those roles. Anyway, I was quite unhappy about all that—and management knew it."

Ferri would not be unhappy for long. A phone call from Italy quite literally changed her life. It was a call from Franco Zeffirelli, the well-known stage director/designer, saying that he was mounting a new production of *Swan Lake* at La Scala, Milan, in which the roles of Odette/Odile would be shared by two dancers. Carla Fracci was one of them. Would Ferri like to be the other? The answer was a resounding yes! Ferri was in heaven. She would be dancing her first classic with Fracci, her early idol, and Zeffirelli would be her director. Moreover, she would be making her La Scala debut—the prodigal's return! As if this were not enough, who should be sitting in the opening night audience but Mikhail Baryshnikov, director of American Ballet Theatre (ABT). Following the performance, Baryshnikov was introduced to Ferri. "Would you like to come to America?" he asked. "Yes—definitely," she replied. And so it was that in August 1985, Allessandra Ferri, then 21-years-old, came to America to join ABT as a principal dancer.

"I had a very hard time when I first came to New York," Ferri recalls. "I had left 6 years behind me in London. I left my friends—wonderful friends. I left because I felt that you only live once, and if opportunity comes, why not take it? I mean, if the greatest dancer of the moment invites you into his company, are you going to refuse? So I came. I also came because I wanted to learn more. Why not work with new teachers and be exposed to a new mentality? But I'll say this: when I came, I was really uptight. I felt a lot of pressure from the company. I was only 21, and everything around me was unfamiliar. I had no friends, no family. The schooling here was different. Being on stage here was different. I felt scared and isolated.

"So I just plunged into work. I realized how far behind I was technically. I worked day and night. The best part was working with Elena Tchernichova, one of our ballet mistresses. Elena has the great gift of being very objective. She knows what each of us can do. She has changed my way of working, given me a lot of strength. So this was the best part of it, and there was a lot of catching up to do."

Although adjusting to her new environment proved difficult, Ferri's place in the company was easily established. Her performances in works such as *Romeo and Juliet, Requiem, Les Sylphides, The Nutcracker,* and *La Bayadère* were both distinguished and compelling. It was clear that here was a charismatic young dancer able to move an audience and give to each of her roles theatrical intonation and edge. But for all that, critics consistently pointed out a general weakness in technique, a factor that riled and depressed the young dancer. Indeed, up to the time of filming the Herbert Ross movie *Dancers* in 1987, Ferri's spirits were considerably dampened by her reviews.

"By the end of the movie, I started to hate dancing," she says. "It was because all I did was try to improve—go to class, rehearse, and go on stage. I was like a machine. I tried desperately to make my body do what everybody said it couldn't. Somehow, I couldn't do it in a vacuum. I needed to feed my head and soul in order to perform. The fact is, I lost heart. I was very lonely and very unhappy with myself. I felt my performances were getting very dry. Finally, after the movie, and when the company went on tour, I injured myself badly and was out of commission."

The leg injury was serious enough to keep Ferri off the stage for 4 months. Feeling it to be a sign, she retreated into herself and realized that what she needed was a complete break from dancing. She flew back to Italy to be with her family. Later, she traveled throughout Italy, looking at art, hearing music, but making it a point not to watch a single ballet performance. Finally, she traveled to London for physical therapy and to renew her many friendships there. In time, the injury healed. Throughout it all, Alessandra Ferri reassessed her young life.

"I came to the conclusion that I had to be a person before being a dancer," she says. "Of course, I would continue to dance, but I felt it didn't make any sense being in one's twenties and not having a life. By having a life, I mean being in love and enjoying one's youth—doing all the things that a 24-year-old girl *should* be doing. In the past, when I was with a man, I couldn't give myself to him completely, because dancing and all that dancing means took all my energy. I always regretted that. There just wasn't enough left over to give to the man next to me. Well, I don't want to ruin my love life. You see, I believe in love. I'm Italian, after all. Love is important to an Italian."

Thus, returning the United States a much happier person, Ferri proceeded to change her life. She became more gregarious; she went out; she met people, including a young rock musician with whom she has, indeed, fallen in love. Working no less hard with Tchernichova and others at ABT, she soon experienced a breakthrough in matters of technique and interpretation, and her latest performances reveal a dancer of far greater authority than before. As the *New York Times* pointed out, following a recent performance of *Giselle,* "Miss Ferri's Giselle has tremendously improved both dramatically and technically."

"I have really changed," Ferri says. "First of all, I'm in love. Secondly, I'm less ambitious that I was. I'm not frantically trying to get to the top anymore. I'm much calmer about all that. I'm much more ambitious for what's inside of me. And I'm much happier at ABT now. I think Misha is a wonderful director. He may not be too good at expressing himself. I mean, he's not too patient with his dancers. But he's an incredibly bright man, and he has a lot to give. These days, he gets especially nervous when he has to dance. When you're nervous, you become a bit selfish. But don't forget, he's had a very bad knee injury that may get worse or stay the same. So he can be a bit short-tempered."

What does Ferri expect of herself as an artist?

"I like to be able to make an audience 'live' something with me. I don't want to be a ballerina for balletomanes. I want people, especially people my own age, to respond to me as a human being—not just to the dancing—not just to an image—but to a person who is living out something on the stage. Aside from that, I have set very high standards with myself. I get terribly depressed if I don't give as much as I know I can give. Then, I feel I'm wasting my time. The point is, dancing should be like life. It should be real and exciting and full of surprises. Watching dance should not be like going to a museum. It should be like going further and further into life."

Mark Morris

Photograph by Tom Brazil

Mark Morris

"Why did you cut off all those beautiful curls?" I asked Mark Morris some weeks ago.

"A couple of reasons," he answered. "I got tired of wearing a ponytail for rehearsals. In performance, it got hot, and the hair stuck to my lips. Also, I was getting too much press about its. It's just hair. It'll grow back if I want it to."

Morris, in red shirt and black pants, was stretched out on a chaise lounge smoking a *Jakarta,* a handmade Indonesian cigarette made of a mixture of tobacco and cloves. Morris is tall and very strong; you might say he's burly. His face, by contrast, is extremely sensitive—a cross between Sean Penn and Boy George. We were talking about his new look—without his curls, he's positively punk—and about the enormous success of the Mark Morris Dance Group.

"There has certainly been a lot of press, and it certainly has been favorable," said Morris. "The good part is that people see the work, and I *get* work. The bad part is that there's a lot of pressure to make a dance to end all dances. Actually, that's not as much a concern as it could be. But it's a lot of responsibility. I do like it that my work is being watched and analyzed."

Morris's work has been watched and analyzed since 1980 when he first formed his group. By 1984, when the company appeared at the Brooklyn Academy of Music's (BAM) New Wave series, dance critics proclaimed him something of a choreographic genius. In the *New Yorker,* Arlene Croce, high priestess of the Balanchine canon, wrote, "He's the clearest illustration we have, at the moment, of the principle of succession and how it works in dance: Each new master assimilates the past in all its variety and becomes our guide to the future." Writing in *Dance Magazine,* Tobi Tobias said, "Morris, at 28, is on just about every dance fan's short list of contemporary choreographers destined for the history books." Reviewing a concert in the *New York Times,* Jennifer Dunning wrote, "Mr. Morris is of the Balanchinian school of dance-making. The dance is of the moment. There are no sets. The costuming, though stylish, is usually street or rehearsal wear. And movement flows from Mr. Morris in wholehearted response to music."

These and other accolades were prompted by choreography so naturally structured and so fresh as to make of dancing a newly minted art form. Although Morris works his dancers hard and the energy level can be dangerously explosive, the formal design of the dances is invariably lucid, if purposely skewed and awkward. Dancers can rush around one another, be propelled forward, cluster together, grapple, separate abruptly, curve into one another, or convolute on the floor, and still suggest an inevitable sense of symmetry and balance. The framework of each dance includes myriad strains of ethnic, modern, ballet, jazz, flamenco, and classical Indian dance. But the eclecticism is inspired. In melding, Morris also dissects. He cuts through a given mode of movement, paring away at nonessentials until a crystalline series of movements are left. He then extends these movements to form a mysterious and unpredictable whole. This is as true in the larger group pieces as it is in the solos or duets, and it is made particularly clear when Morris himself takes center stage.

A remarkable performer with wide experience, Morris in the throes of one of his own pieces is transformed into a sly and sinewy instrument able to suggest the purities as well as the incongruities of dance. There is something slightly outrageous about his stage persona, as if he didn't quite belong there, as if he wandered in from some other planet. There's a touch of the ungainly about Morris—something too big and exaggerated for comfort. But it is precisely the awkward logic of his *way* of moving that proves so riveting. And, in a modified way, all his dancers assume some of Morris's own weirdly effective characteristics.

At the base of it all is the music. As it was with Balanchine, music is the ground Morris walks on. His response to it is so acute that he dares to go from the sublime to the ridiculous: from massive Handel choruses to a banal setting of Joyce Kilmer's *Trees*; from Vivaldi, Purcell, and Boccherini to Henry Cowell, Shostakovich, and the Violent Femmes, Morris seems to reside within the music. He is not a listener, but a participant in its actual making. The pulse of the music is the heartbeat of each dance. Again, the dancers don't dance *to* the music: they are *in* the music. They don't hear it: they *are* it. This is why the dances seem predestined yet new. Few choreographers respond to music as viscerally as Morris. Music taught him how to choreograph.

Morris was born on August 29, 1956, in Seattle, Washington. Seattle is where he still lives and works, preferring his home roots to the dance-hustling atmosphere of New York, where, in fact, he had spent several years as a working dancer.

When he was 6, Morris decided he liked moving to music. He didn't know it was called dancing. When he was alone, he'd dress himself in sheets and do extensive solos. One was to Saint-Saën's *Danse Macabre;* another was to Tchaikovsky's *1812 Overture.* He made up stories to go with the movements—the kind, he says, he still makes up today. His father was a high-school teacher who died when Morris was 16. His mother loved dance, particularly flamenco. He has two older sisters. His earliest exposures to dance were movie musicals and José Greco. Spanish dance became his passion.

At age 9, he began a weekly flamenco class with Verla Flowers, who had studied with Mateo and La Argentinita. Later, he began formal training with Perry Brunson, a noted ballet teacher in Seattle. By age 13, he had joined a semiprofessional group called the Koledo Balkan Dance Ensemble, with which he performed Bulgarian and Yugoslavian dances. Upon graduation from high school, Morris knew he would be a dancer and, hopefully, a flamenco dancer. To that end, he traveled to Spain in search of teachers. He was 17.

"I met a teacher in Madrid and started doing a lot of jota," Morris said. "All the jota one sees is highly balleticized, but this teacher was into heavy jota. He taught class just with castanets and sang jotas. You did this really wild calisthenic warmup, and then you did the dances. You were in rope shoes—you were all sickled and wild—sort of simian. It was great! I did that more than flamenco, because I saw that the flamenco scene in Spain had really become quite awful—vulgar, even. Only once in a while did you find a pearl. Anyway, the big decision was whether to become a flamenco dancer or another kind of dancer. Well, I didn't become a flamenco dancer, mostly because I couldn't live in Spain any longer than I did; I lived there for 11 months.

"You see, I was just coming out then, and Spain is incredibly homophobic. I mean, the night life is highly clandestine, although the gay community in Madrid was very supportive. There weren't any gay bars there. But there were regular meeting houses for everyone, and then, after a certain hour, it was known that they turned into gay bars. Anyway, the homophobic stuff really got to me. I mean, you could get arrested just for looking too flamboyant. Well, I wasn't going to pass, because I don't believe in that. So, I came back, returned to Seattle, and continued studying with Perry Brunson. I worked with him for another 9 months. I got very strong and very determined. Perry's classes were incredibly grueling. He was also quite fascistic. So, we all got very strong, but developed rather oddly. Anatomically, we were a mess; we all had strange placement and moved with a sort of consti-pated action. It took a couple of years to get over that."

In January, 1976, Morris moved to New York. He took classes with Maggie Black and worked intensively with Marjorie Mussman and later with Joselyn Lorenz. As a talented dancer, he felt he could move into either ballet or modern dance. "I figured, altruistically, that a really good dancer should be able to do anything. This is true. But it's also impossible, improbable, impractical, and, finally, diluting. I veered into modern dance."

For the next 5 years, Morris danced with the companies of Eliot

Feld, Lar Lubovitch, Twyla Tharp, Hannah Kahn, and Laura Dean. Speaking candidly, he briefly described his experiences with these choreographers.

On Eliot Feld: "It was a good beginning, because it was a real job. We toured a lot. We had to know a lot of pieces, whether we danced them or not. There were a lot of good dancers. And Eliot is brilliant. Of course, everyone knows he's difficult. Frankly, I didn't like the way he treated people, it was just a little too debasing. But I liked his dances. He devised incredible partner work. I remember certain leverages that were really good. I left Eliot when I started liking his dances less. But I learned a lot from him. Eliot and I liked each other, but we had trouble. We both had opinions."

On Lar Lubovitch: "I joined Lar's company practically the moment I left Eliot's. It seemed exactly how I wanted to dance. It felt great. I loved the way Lar spirited the dances—the way they came into being. Unfortunately, Lar didn't create too many dances during the year or so I was with him, and I didn't want to do the same pieces all the time. In 1978, I felt it was time to *not* dance with Lar anymore. I was thinking of dances of my own. And, I was getting impatient."

On Twyla Tharp: "I worked for Twyla for about a month. I was an extra for the dances she made for the movie *Hair*. But I was wrong for her company. I like Twyla's work a lot. I think she's a great choreographer, but I don't like what she does now. I like how her dances are built, but I don't like what they mean; I don't like her message. I think it's condescending and false. I don't think the work she does is false—I know that she means it. But I think it's kind of mean-spirited. The early stuff always had an edge of hostility that I really liked, but it has turned into a kind of bitterness which I don't like. Still, she's very thorough."

On Hannah Kahn: "I hadn't seen her dances at all when I joined her company—I just performed them. I was never so challenged physically and, especially, mentally. It's very, very difficult work. You have to be smart and good to do it. It felt great to finally master that stuff. But what's weird, is that when you *see* it, it's one big wash. It's all on one level. It's so ornate and so filigreed that what is incredibly interesting and detailed at the beginning of a concert, becomes static by the end. So, I liked dancing her pieces more than watching them. Hannah is highly musical, and her stuff is beautifully structured."

On Laura Dean: "When I first saw her pieces, right after I came to New York, I was completely blown away. They were great! It was a company that had been together a long time, and I was the new member. It was very, very hard work, and very satisfying and rewarding. And it was great touring New Zealand, Indonesia, and India. Also, I met Erin Matthiessen in the company, fell in love, and moved in with him.

After a while, he and I got fired. We were replaced by 18-year-old kids who wouldn't talk back. It was just as well, because when we left, Laura was working on a piece called *Sky Light,* which I didn't like at all. I felt she was changing the focus of her work—which I had loved before. The work was suddenly presentational—it was 'kick here, run over there, balance there for a long time.' I didn't like it. But in the middle of all that, we did *Timpany,* which is a great dance."

Morris returned to dance with the Lubovitch company for some 8 months, touring throughout Asia. It was the last company he would work for. In 1980, he formed the Mark Morris Dance Group. The repertory consisted of dances he had choreographed while still in his teens, as well as more current works. His first concert was held at the Merce Cunningham studio.

"I formed a company reluctantly," Morris said. "What I wanted to do was quite Utopian—to gather a group of friends and put on a show. So, my first company was made up of people from class, from Lar's company, and Laura's company. Hannah Kahn was in it. It was a low-stress situation—no board of directors, no letterhead. Then, the next year, I formed another company—the company I have now—and we performed at the Dance Theater Workshop (DTW) for 3 successive years, 1981 to 1983. Then we did the BAM concert in 1984 and the DTW season in December of 1985. I have 13 dancers. They're brilliant. They're adults. It's a pretty old group of dancers. I'm in charge, and I'm very demanding. Some of the pieces are actually dangerous. I work everybody very hard. But we all like one another."

How does Morris choreograph? How do the dances come out looking the way they do? What are the movements about? What is the propelling motivation?

"First of all, let's talk about George Balanchine. When I finally saw the New York City Ballet performing, I just about passed out. What I learned from Balanchine is that you can do whatever you want. Even if you don't like a piece of his, he's always right. And he's got a certain decorum that I find just so impressive. I read a Balanchine quote the other day, about music being an aquarium, which is such a great image! And the idea that if you hate a dance, just close your eyes and listen to the music. That's so right *on*! And I learn things just by watching Suzanne Farrell dance. Though she may have been dancing a certain piece for 10 years, she's still perpetually astonishing. I don't know what it is. She has a spontaneity that I can't believe; I can't believe she can pull it off *all* the time. She dances with the speed of thought. And though the form of the piece is evident, and she knows what it is, she's continually surprising. She just amazes me!

"So, that's something I aim for—that incredible spontaneity. As for how I create my dances—well, it's assimilation. Having dealt with all those very, very difficult Bulgarian dances that I was trained in, having had to master all those incredible internal rhythms—looking as though you quiver, but it's really internal—has gone into some of my dances. Also, dancing while holding hands or touching someone actually changes everything about how everybody dances. And that's gone into some of my dances.

"My structure comes from the structure of the music I use. In a way, the dances become musical visualizations—and I like that. Or, I'll take a rhythmic motif that appears somewhere in the music, and I'll make up a step that echoes it. Then, I'll put that same step in places where it doesn't belong—or change the rhythm of it. And it can become another movement later on. It's an artifice that allows me to tie a piece of dancing together in the way I feel the music is tied together—like the tonal architecture that you don't hear immediately, but understand if you listen to a piece for a long time. So, I try to make people able to see and hear that at the same time. It requires different things to happen physically and musically.

"Often, my things look clichéd. But clichés were all true at one time. I did a piece once called *Ten Suggestions* to Tcherepnin's *Piano Bagatelles;* I just wanted it to be a musical visualization. That was the goal. It was, 'This sounds like this, so why not do just *that*?' I mean, look at Balanchine's *Liebeslieder Walzer.* They're lovely waltzes. That's what they are. So why move chairs around in black and white leotards to that sort of music? What you do with Brahms waltzes is to wear gloves and kiss hands. It doesn't mean it's corny. It means it's true. So that's what I do, too. What I'm saying is, what do you do with a hoop? You jump through it. What do you do with a ribbon? You swirl it. What do you do with a chair? You sit on it.

"So I go for a certain reality, which sometimes comes out looking peculiar. I feel that now I'm beginning to say what I want. I always could put steps together, but now pieces are less step-oriented—more frightening. It sometimes bothers me that people laugh at my dances. I know that people laugh for a lot of different reasons. I'm not insulted, but I'm often surprised. The intent is to be true, not to be funny."

Despite his absence from the New York dance scene, Morris achieved the status of a celebrity—a role he relishes. "I like being in the public eye, because I feel I have something to say," he explains. Far more significantly, he's become the country's hottest young choreographer, and major companies are commissioning works. The demand increased when, in 1986, public television's *Dance in America* series broadcast a 90-minute program devoted to his works.

In 1986 alone, Morris choreographed *Mort subite* for the Boston

Ballet, *Soap Powders and Detergents* and *Striptease* for the Mark Morris Dance Group (both of which, like his 1984 *Championship Wrestling*, were based on essays by Roland Barthes), *The Dance of the Seven Veils* for the Seattle Opera's production of *Salomé*, an extended work to Pergolesi's *Stabat Mater* for the Brooklyn Academy of Music's 1986–1987 season, and *Esteemed Guests* for the Joffrey Ballet. Since then, he created *Drink To Me Only With Thine Eyes* for ABT; conceived the movement for director Peter Sellars's controversial 1987 BAM production, *Nixon In China;* choreographed *Orpheus and Eurydice* for the Seattle Opera; and—also for the Seattle Opera—made his directorial debut with *Die Fledermaus.*

In the fall of 1987, the Mark Morris Group began a 3-year engagement as the resident dance company of the *Théâtre Royal de la Monnaie* in Brussels, the former home of Maurice Béjart's Ballet of the Twentieth Century.

Mark Morris is nothing if not clear-eyed about his goals. "I'm interested in mastery," he says. "Mastery in the sense of a Japanese National Living Treasure practicing some incredibly obscure art form that nobody knows about anymore, like applying gold leaf or dyeing things indigo or denting a pot so it's not perfect. I'm talking about real mastery, where nothing else matters. So, when I'm working on a dance, *that's* what I want—*that's* what I'm after."

Photograph by Costas

Heather Watts

Do complex people make interesting dancers? Judging by the work of Heather Watts, one of the New York City Ballet's most idiosyncratic soloists, the answer is a resounding "Yes." Since her entry into the company in 1970, Watts has consistently offered the image of a dancer imbued with a highly individualistic approach to the Balanchine/Robbins aesthetic.

As a wiry youngster in the corps of which she was a member for 7 years, Watts produced an amalgam of amibuously executed movements, not always tied to the singular vision of the choreography at hand. It was never a matter of deviation from the steps, however, but rather a question of intonation. Some inner mechanism, seemingly more tied to the mind than to the body, would find the dancer creating a tensile thrust of legs, arms, and torso that often overintensified a pirouette, an arabesque, or a jump. It gave notice of Watts's very particular sense of urgency, and the result was a stark, often austere, highly concentrated presence that decidedly engaged the eye.

To see Watts in motion during her early corps years was to be in touch with a dancer who insisted on achieving clarity on her own terms. It was a clarity made evident through subtle yet provocative exaggeration—an extra stop released, a moment in time stretched and deepened, a gesture savored. These quixotic liberties, later to coalesce into the Watts style, might momentarily unsettle the fluidity of a corps variation, but never destroyed it. Then as now, whatever she did was invariably interesting. This interest continued as one observed her face with its finely molded features, its prominent brow, its cool, impervious expression.

Watts has emerged as one of the City Ballet's most fascinating artists. She elicits strong response by virtue of eccentricities that heighten the meaning and dimension of any ballet she performs. Again, it is never a question of veering from the steps, but simply a matter of striving for personal discovery. A strong, clean technician, Watts commands attention through her boldness of attack and through the emotional components in her dancing that allow for an ever increasing freedom of interpretation.

When she was promoted to soloist in May, 1978, she danced leading roles in Balanchine's *Nutcracker, Symphony in C, Tchaikovsky Pas de Deux, Concerto Barocco, Stars and Stripes, Jewels, Vienna Waltzes, A Midsummer Night's Dream,* and *Orpheus,* as well as Robbins's *The Cage* and *The Four Seasons.* Her appearances in Peter Martins's first ballet, *Calcium Light Night* (1978), and in his second major ballet, *Giardino di Scarlatti* (1979), found Watts receiving very particular attention. Her individuality, both as a person and as a dancer, came brilliantly to the fore, and the press took note. As *Time* magazine put it, "Heather Watts is a lithe wire of a woman who radiates both sensuality and wit on stage ... A lady with magnetism." Watts has gone on to dance leading roles in over twenty ballets. They include Balanchine's *Davidsbündlertänze, Bugaku, Liebeslieder Walzer, Agon,* and the Second and Third Movements of *Brahms-Schoenberg Quartet,* and Martins's *Suite from L'Histoire du Soldat, Concerto for Two Solo Pianos, Tango, Songs of the Auvergne,* and *Ecstatic Orange.*

The specifics of her style center on a physical vocabulary that finds her negotiating choreographic intent with an arresting combination of lyricism and tension. Her phrasing is at once muscular, lean, and loose. The movements are stretched out, often to the point of slight awkwardness. And yet, the look of it works. There's logic in it. Watching Watts dance, one senses a refreshing inevitability in the contour and progression of her approach.

In *Concerto Barocco,* for example, Watts's alluring angularity invests the ballet with an etched, silver-point radiance. It is abstract classicism invaded by a geometry all its own. In Martins's *Calcium Light Night,* the definition and fabric of her physicality is brought into particular focus. The broad shoulders, thin torso, and long, beautiful legs convey the terseness and quirkiness of the choreography, and Watts's gaunt malleability is put to stunning use. In her pas de deux with Daniel Duell, she is, in turn, stretched, slid, coiled, and lifted in ways that give an essentially dramatic and violent encounter a resonance of macabre wit. She seems possessed, but possessed by a benevolent demon that goads and propels her into being a mock-serious sorceress.

Watts has been called a quirky dancer. The fact is, she is not so much quirky as daring. She resists the expected despite her enormous allegiance to the lessons of Balanchine, and even she herself is surprised by the results. In a way, she filters the Balanchine precepts of speed, musicality, and risk through a sensibility that transforms them into a personal vision. It is this vision (perhaps still unconsciously perceived) that sets her so beguilingly apart.

Upon meeting Watts in person, one becomes immediately aware of her acute sensitivity, one that renders her wary of persons in search of revelations. Because she is trusting and emotional, she is doubly guarded. Still, there are many areas of accessibility. For example, she will talk freely about the fact that as a youngster she was something of a "bad kid."

"It's true! I was bratty and precocious. I talked too much and chewed gum. Whatever was wrong, I would do. I was very energetic, very lively, almost hyperactive. I wasn't mean, but I was a little gang-leader ... and the gang was always in trouble!"

Watts was referring to her high school years spent in Chatsworth, near Los Angeles, California, where she was born on September 27, 1953. Her father was formerly a space engineer but has since become involved in laser fusion as part of an energy program being conducted in California. Her mother is an Englishwoman, born in Leeds, who currently writes for a San Fernando Valley newspaper. She has two brothers and a sister.

Of her childhood, she says, "I was quite sick as a child. I had a bad bout with rheumatic fever at 7, and at 9 I contracted mononucleosis. Taking ballet lessons was a way to gain strength. Of course, what I *really* wanted to be was a movie star. My mother said, 'Well, if you want to be a movie star, we'll have to get you acting lessons.' And she took me to an acting teacher. He was a wonderful man, but he didn't really know what to do with me. He told my mother: 'There's no way to tell at 10. Heather certainly has a dramatic streak, but she's very clumsy. Why not give her ballet lessons instead?'

"And so, off I went to ballet school which was in Chatsworth and quite close to where we lived. My teacher there was Sheila Rozann; she was wonderful, very progressive and very Balanchine-oriented. She was very involved with technique and the beauty of dancing. Well, I had been studying with Miss Rozann for about 5 or 6 months when the New York City Ballet came to the Greek Theater in LA. That was in 1964, and among the works they were performing was *A Midsummer Night's Dream.* They needed children, so Sheila Rozann took all her little girls and drove them to the theater for an audition. I was already 11 and tall for my age, but I got chosen. I was one of the four big bugs that carries Oberon's cape, and Oberon was Edward Villella!

"Right then and there I fell in love with Eddie. He was so exciting, so glamorous, so beautiful! And the role of Titania was danced by Suzanne Farrell. Well, I fell in love with her, too. There was a moment when some of us children knelt before her, and I saw all those diamonds and rhinestones and I saw her beauty ... those eyes! And I saw these pink satin pointe shoes; it was all too much! From that moment on, I knew I wanted to be a dancer, and I wanted to be a dancer with the New York City Ballet."

While the City Ballet was performing in Los Angeles, George Balanchine himself visited Sheila Rozann's ballet classes and considered her school worthy of funding by the Ford Foundation. The following spring, Diana Adams, a principal dancer with the company, visited the school and selected a number of gifted students for Ford Foundation Scholarship grants which would pay for their ballet lessons. Eleven-year-old Watts was among them. One year later, another City Ballet ballerina, Violette Verdy, came to visit Sheila Rozann's school and taught classes for a period of 2 weeks. Miss Verdy quickly noted Watts's potential and suggested to Heather's mother that she allow her daughter to visit New York during the summer months so that she might take classes at the School of American Ballet (SAB). Mrs. Watts felt that it was too soon for Heather to live in New York on her own, but agreed to allow her to go the following year.

"I came to New York at 13. I came with another girl and her mother. It was incredible. I mean, I had never been out of California and had never been in an airplane. I just loved it all. It was the summer of 1967, and my teachers at SAB were Stanley Williams, André Eglevsky, Alexandra Danilova, and Patricia Neary. They had five divisions at the school and I was put in the fourth, which was great honor considering the fact that I couldn't even stand up! I was the weakest thing you'd ever seen. My legs were like toothpicks. But I loved the classes. I loved Stanley and Eglevsky and Danilova. And I had pas de deux class for the very first time and I'd never even *seen* boy dancers in a class. I remember seeing little 12-year-old Fernando Bujones doing the most amazing things. I had never seen anyone dance so *neatly.*"

The SAB thought enough of Watts's capabilities to ask her to stay on, but the girl's parents still deemed her too young to be on her own. There would be the following summer and the summer after that. In the meantime, there was regular schooling to think about. At 15, Watts would enter high school, and dancing would have to be fit in accordingly. But the youngster fell into a slight state of depression. Indeed, upon her return to California, she gave up her dance studies entirely. This period of inactivity lasted for nearly a year. Watts was going through her "bad kid" phase. Soon she realized that dancing was still in her blood, and she quickly resolved to resume her studies. She began training with a teacher named Natalie Clare who taught ballet classes in North Hollywood.

"I went to Natalie Clare in a bad state. The fact was, I didn't really know whether or not I wanted to dance. But Miss Clare was very helpful and encouraged me in a very quiet and wonderful way. She helped me to overcome my shyness and tried to tell me to be happy with myself. She made me feel good about what I did, and she didn't push me beyond my capabilities, which is something many teachers do. Anyway, she pulled me out of my torpor, and at one point, I even danced in the corps of her small company, which is called Ballet La Jeunesse. I appeared in *Serenade;* it was my very first Balanchine ballet."

It had become clear to each of her California teachers—Sheila Rozann, Natalie Clare, as well as the late Carmelita Maracci, with whom Watts had trained briefly—that dancing could indeed become the girl's career. Finally, winning her parents' consent, Watts traveled to New York and resumed her classes at the School of American Ballet. She would henceforth live in New York and continue her regular schooling at the Professional Children's School (PCS). As it turned out, her new-found freedom contrived to bring out the renegade in her, that "bratty kid" again reared her pretty head.

"For one thing, I absolutely hated going to the Professional Children's School. I thought it was horrible. Back home, I had been in a program called AE—Academically Enriched classes—suddenly, I was shoved into this ghastly French I and a nasty history class that made no sense. There was nothing interesting about what I was doing at PCS. So, I skipped a lot of classes and, I'm sorry to say, I also skipped a lot of my ballet classes. It was a teenage thing ... all that sudden freedom.

"The teachers at the School of American Ballet thought I was talented, but they soon realized that I also spelled trouble. I'd talk loudly; I didn't finish exercises. If I didn't like the way I did a step in the center, I'd just stop and walk to the back. If I didn't like a class, what was the point? The fact is, I didn't respect discipline. I didn't respect older people. Balanchine, yes. But the other Russians ... well, I thought: 'Who cares if I don't finish a class, who cares if I chew gum, who cares if I don't curtsy at the end of class?' It all seemed stupid to me.

"At one point, the school threatened to send me home until I became a little more mature. They called my parents and, of course, I got hysterical and became very contrite because I really *did* love SAB. All I wanted out of life was the New York City Ballet! I was smart enough to know that if I got kicked out of the school as a scholarship student, I'd never get into the company. But I went on being a mess. I remember being kicked out of an Eglevsky class—Mr. Balanchine was called, and he came over to the school and talked to me. He said, 'You know, dear, you have to be nice. You have to respect authority. You must go and watch other classes. Watch Gelsey Kirkland. If you hear she's in class, go watch her. Watch how her feet work. And watch Suzanne ... learn from her.' He encouraged me about ballet. And he wasn't soupy—just very caring and straightforward.

"Of course, I was worried about all this, but I thought; 'Hey, they're all fussing over me!' I know that sounds horrible, but I *did* get a lot of attention. Still, I wasn't promoted the following year. I wasn't moved up to D class, and I was almost 17! In the meantime, I had quit going to the Professional Children's School. I just couldn't stand it. So I began correspondence courses, and finally, got my high school diploma at 19. But not being promoted to D class was the real trauma, because it was from D class that you got into the company.

"You see, I had this absolute conviction that once I got into the company, I would dance ... *magically!* Of course, I knew very well that there was no reason for me to get into the company. I wasn't ready. But I was stupidly convinced that once I'd dance in the company, everything would fall into place."

Indeed, as Heather Watts saw it, entering the company would make her whole, both as a person and a dancer. And George Balanchine in his wisdom understood the girl's dilemma. Canny and perceptive about dancers, the choreographer was fully aware of Watts's intrinsic potential and resolved to formulate a plan. In 1970, the dancer was moved to D class and also appeared in a workshop production of a piece choreographed by Richard Tanner, a dancer with the company. That season, the ballet was taken into the repertory—minus Watts. Still, she *was* offered a contract, and her greatest wish had come true. She was now a member of the New York City Ballet. What the dancer did not know was that the contract seemed the only way for management to deal with her productively. It seemed the only way to get her to work more seriously. She would be a member of the corps, but actual performances were another matter.

"I thought that once I got into the company I would get to dance. I mean, Bart Cook and Tracy Bennett and Victor Castelli all got in when I did, and they started dancing immediately. Well, not me! I couldn't believe it. Finally, Mr. Balanchine came to me and said, 'No, dear, I don't really want you to dance yet. I want you to take my class. Come around, watch, learn, absorb. You can do a few things if we need you, but really, you're here to get strong and to learn how to dance."

"Well, this went on for 2 years! I was demoralized. I actually lost my sense of dedication. I would stay out late and sleep late. I didn't take Mr. Balanchine's classes and, again, I was a mess. Every once in a while I would be called to do a few things, like *Swan Lake* and *Stars and Stripes,* but that was about *it.*"

By the age of 19, Heather Watts was finally given more to do, and she readily assimilated herself into the company. Yet it was a struggle. In her heart she knew that simply being a member of the New York City Ballet did not mean instant success and stardom. There was still a great deal to learn. When Watts turned 20, panic overtook her.

"I got scared at 20. I got desperate. I felt I had to pull myself together, because I really *did* want to be a good dancer. So, I began taking lots and lots of Mr. B.'s classes, and immediately he was very receptive. Look, I was in the corps for 7 years, but I did nothing for 4 of them. It was getting ridiculous. Well, little by little, things improved. I was put in *Episodes*. I got a demi-soloist part in *Symphony in C*. I danced in *Allegro Brilliante* and *Goldberg Variations*. Still, I considered myself very unmusical. Everyone in the company was always saying: 'Heather, you're late! You're off the music! You have no energy!'

"And so I worked ... *really* worked. I mean, Gelsey Kirkland was with us dancing the lead in *Theme* at 21! I was 20 and not even good enough to be in the corps of *Theme!* I had to do something. I had to learn exactly what Mr. B. meant by a correction. I had to think and concentrate and understand. You see, more than anything in my life, I wanted to please him. And this need to please Mr. Balanchine was the turning point in my dancing. I know we all say that we should dance for ourselves, but I really wanted to dance for *him*."

Between 1974 and 1978, Watts progressed at an astonishing pace. Her motivation to dance deepened, and her work assumed scope and dimension. A new-found exhilaration propelled her into self-discovery. She was learning, thinking, and, above all, working. Balanchine took note, and in 1978, Heather Watts was promoted to the rank of soloist.

She danced the lead in Robbins's *The Cage*, performed leading roles in *Goldberg Variations* and *Scherzo Fantastique;* she appeared in Balanchine's *Suite No. 3, Raymonda Variations, Four Temperaments* and, to her own astonishment, was cast in the "Rubies" section of *Jewels*.

"When I saw my name posted for 'Rubies', I said *What?!* I'm not fast; I'm not funny; and I have never even been in the corps of this ballet. It was strange, but somehow it settled in my mind the question that was gnawing at me: Can I really dance? Well, I did 'Rubies' and it went well, and I thought, Yes, maybe I *can* dance. Then, *Brahms-Schoenberg* came along—this third movement, which is very romantic, very simple, very classical, very gorgeous—and I was stunned. I realized that I could do *that* too. Maybe I'm not just for *Episodes* and *Cage*. Maybe there are other parts for me. And so it went. I danced the pas de deux in *Symphony in Three Movements*. Suddenly, I realized that I could do the leotard ballets even better than before. I could bring more to them. I didn't have to rely on being weird. I could make accents with things other than ginches.* I could just *dance*. And it was all Mr. B.'s doing, because Mr. B. always says, 'Just dance!'

---

*A "ginch" is Suzanne Farrell's trademark gesture, a slight glance over the shoulder. Gelsey Kirkland describes it as epitomizing "animal magnetism."

"It was such a revelation, because I realized that I wasn't limited—that I could be *everything*. I mean, I used to look at Allegra Kent, and that's all I wanted to be. I wanted to *be* her. I wanted to dance like her; I wanted to look like her. I wanted those feet, those legs. But that was wrong, because as long as I felt that way, I was limiting myself. Young dancers tend to do that, but they mustn't. They mustn't say, 'I'm a soubrette or I'm lyrical or I'm classical.' That only limits you. What they must say is, 'I *dance!*'"

In her early years in the corps, Heather Watts had ample occasion to note the spectacular presence of Peter Martins, a principal with the company. The handsome, blond Danish dancer offered the image of pure classicism, and his artistry was matched by a personality of enormous charm and wit. Clearly, he was romance personified, and Watts, like many another corps girl, was captivated. For his part, Martins must have been aware of the thin, highly sensitive girl undergoing her various inner struggles. The two eventually met, and, in time, began to share their life together.

"Peter and I have been together for years. It's been on and off, but it's been a long time. We're not exactly the easiest people, but, somehow, we've managed to get along. Actually, it's amazing, because we spend 12 hours a day at the City Ballet, and you'd think we'd want to get away from it. But you see, we both love the company. It's our life. We talk endlessly about the company, if we like a particular dancer, or if a ballet is really great. I'm sure people must think we're loony, because we can spend hours fighting over these things.

"We're both quite moody. I mean, Peter is usually easygoing, but he can also be very difficult. Of course, I'm the extremist. I'm either too happy or too sad. Peter has always tried to temper my moods. If I'm sad about something, he'll say, 'Don't overdramatize. You'll get over it.' If I'm elated about something, he'll say, 'Don't be too happy; it might not happen.' So he tempers me."

Heather Watts talked about the genesis of Peter Martins's first ballet, *Calcium Light Night,* set to the music of Charles Ives: "*Calcium* was begun during the City Ballet orchestra strike in 1977. Peter had created four short variations for Daniel Duell. When I saw them I was stunned. I thought they were wonderful, and I thought Danny was incredible. Mr. Balanchine saw what Peter was doing and asked him, 'Why don't you add a girl?' Well, Peter must have asked him who might be suitable. Mr. B. said, 'You need to work with someone whose body you know.' So Peter chose me, not because we knew each other, but because he's always liked my dancing. When we began to work on the pas de deux, he started giving me steps that I thought were horrendous. There was no way I could do them. We fought like cats and dogs.

Peter kept saying that I *could* do them, but that if I didn't *want* to do them, he'd get someone else. Anyway, it all simmered down and began to work. I think that part of the success of *Calcium* was not so much the steps as the look and the idea. The pas de deux has a very definite idea. Peter always liked the pas de deux I did in *Episodes*. You know, the manipulative things, the man moving the woman to dance. Although *Calcium* is not a take-off on *Episodes,* it's the same idea. Danny moves me and moves me again; it's weird and has a special look. Well, I think *Calcium* is a beautiful work and I love dancing it."

The future holds much in store for Heather Watts. So far, she has proven herself in major Balanchine, Robbins, and Martins roles, and there have been extraordinary highlights. In 1979, she was promoted to principal dancer and soon thereafter was chosen to perform the "Rubies" section of *Jewels* at the White House, as part of the nationally televised program *Live from the White House.* Her partner for the occasion was Mikhail Baryshnikov. Watts's parents were on hand to witness their daughter perform for the President of the United States. Watts's other television appearances include *Bournonville Dances, The Magic Flute, Agon,* and *A Choreographer's Notebook* for public television's *Dance in America* series. In 1985, she received the *Dance Magazine* award and was also a recipient of the New York Public Library's first annual "Lions of the Performing Arts" award.

With it all, Heather Watts still feels oddly insecure ... perhaps amazed at her good fortune, unable to believe it. What she *is* secure about and totally committed to is the New York City Ballet, the place she had always wanted to be, the symbol of excellence she had always strived for.

"All I want is to dance with the City Ballet. There is nothing else I want to do. I don't want to dance *Giselle* with American Ballet Theatre. I don't want to be a guest in Europe. This is where I want to be and this is what I want to do. I wanted to work with Mr. Balanchine. I wanted to do his ballets. That's *it.* Does that sound strange? Well, it isn't, because it's all I *really* care about."

Arthur Mitchell

Photograph Courtesy of Susan Bloch and Company

Arthur Mitchell

On a pretty tree-lined street in Harlem, an inconspicuous brick building bears a modest sign reading "The Dance Theatre of Harlem" (DTH). This unprepossessing yet solid two-storied structure on New York's 152nd Street is the home of the world's only ballet company comprised almost entirely of classically trained black dancers—a cultural phenomenon that has thrillingly defied the longstanding notion that blacks cannot perform classical ballet.

Within its walls, dance activity is rampant and music is heard everywhere. Housing the company, as well as its school, these friendly, well-organized quarters include six studios in which daily classes are held and where the company itself rehearses. There is a bustling costume shop, a busy library containing hundreds of books and periodicals on dance, and a series of tiny offices, the most cluttered and active of which belongs to company director Arthur Mitchell.

As in ballet schools the world over, dancers in leotards, tights, leg-warmers, and colorful headbands fill the halls and studios. But at DTH, the atmosphere is charged with a particular sense of purpose, for this is a generation of black dancers entrusted with a singular mission: to excel in and conquer a field that has been virtually closed to them and to make it known that the black classical dancer has indeed arrived. One feels this pride and dedication whether observing a class of 8-year-olds carefully negotiating their *pliés* and *tendus* or some 40 company members rehearsing a George Balanchine or Agnes de Mille classic. It can be seen in the sleek and tensile thrust of the men's audacious leaps and jumps and in the women's secure and pliable bearing. And it can be felt in the teachers and ballet masters whose task it is to make the once unheard of an undisputed reality.

Today, DTH, founded in 1969 by Arthur Mitchell (once the only black dancer in the prestigious New York City Ballet), has gained international stature and is considered among the world's major American ballet companies.

It is unquestionably an appetite for risk that propelled Mitchell into a venture fraught with obstacles and for which there had been little precedent. The short-lived First Negro Classical Ballet Company, formed by the British-born white dancer Aubrey Hitchens in the late 1940s, proved a meager stepping stone in a profession that continued to insist that black dancers were not built along the rarefied lines required in classical dance. The assumption had always been that blacks could only excel in Afro-ethnic, Caribbean, jazz, tap, and modern dance. Although major black artists such as Katherine Dunham and Alvin Ailey formed companies that brilliantly celebrated some of these unique dance styles, no black dancer had ever attempted to launch an all-black classical ballet company until Mitchell, a man of daunting determination and boundless energy, found a way.

"It's not that I woke up one morning and got this great emotional feeling and said, 'I'm going to start a company,'" said Mitchell, in his office at DTH. "What *did* happen was that back in 1968, I was off to Brazil at the invitation of the State Department to form a Brazilian ballet company. In fact, I had been commuting between New York and Rio de Janeiro for about 2 years, when, on that last trip, the news came that Martin Luther King had been assassinated. Well, I got very upset and said to myself, 'This is silly! Why am I making these 9-hour trips around the world building ballet companies? I should be doing this at home!'"

At the time, Mitchell was still performing as principal dancer with the New York City Ballet, which he had joined in 1956. Although he would continue dancing with the company until 1971, he began to formulate ways of bringing classical dance to underprivileged youngsters in Harlem who, he felt, needed only the encouragement, the opportunity, and the place to make ballet study possible. Following the precepts of his mentor, George Balanchine, director of the New York City Ballet, Mitchell knew that without a school—a training ground—no lasting company could exist.

"I took my own money and rented a garage on St. Nicholas Avenue in Harlem," Mitchell continued. "I laid down a new floor and began teaching class. I started with 30 students, and by the end of that summer there were 400 kids in the program. Tuition was 50 cents for children under 12 and a dollar for the rest. Well, everyone thought I had gone off my rocker when I said I'd start a ballet program up in Harlem. They said that black kids wouldn't take to the discipline, wouldn't be able to relate to it, wouldn't understand it. And in the Harlem community people said, 'Why is he up here? A ballet dancer? We never heard of a black ballet dancer! Is it a real estate deal? Is it a political deal? Is he an Uncle Tom? Is he a pawn for downtown?' All sorts of things came into play. Of course, they were wrong. Finally, the program was so successful that we had to move to larger quarters and, eventually, through a grant from Mrs. Alva Gimbel, we acquired and renovated the building we're in now."

The success of Mitchell's school was such that he was soon able to attract well-known teachers, including the late Karel Shook (1920–1975), one of the world's finest classical pedagogues, whom Mitchell recruited from Holland and who remained to become DTH's codirector. Said Mr. Shook: "Neither Arthur nor I wanted to prove that black people could do ballet. We knew they could, although myth had it that they couldn't. People said that their backs were built the wrong way or that their behinds were too big. But black people *can* do ballet, because ballet is nonethnic. So, we didn't want to prove that it *could* happen, we just *wanted* it to happen."

"You see," Mitchell added, "we weren't championing a cause, because when you're out on stage, it doesn't matter what color you are. The question is: Who is the best dancer? I had to *show* that to the world rather than *tell* them about it. I said, 'Let's put black classical dancers on the stage and let people see it!'"

Although it takes about 10 years to train a classical dancer, Mitchell's aim was to allow his dancers to perform almost immediately—to learn by doing—to place them on the stage in a sink-or-swim situation. Thus, the most talented survived and garnered valuable performing experience even as they continued to pursue their classroom training. It was this growth through experience that contributed to the company's rapid rise and success. The luminous, quicksilver presence of each of the company's dancers must, in part, be attributed to the immediacy of their approach to the very act of dancing. Indeed, in a company of 42 dancers, the hallmark has always been unbridled energy and *éclat* wedded to technical refinement and expressiveness.

In matters of repertory—the backbone of any company—DTH's classical base has been extended to encompass a wide variety of styles. The company performs the abstract, neoclassical masterpieces of George Balanchine, notably *Agon, The Four Temperaments, Concerto Barocco, Allegro Brillante,* and *Square Dance,* and such classics as *Swan Lake* (Act II), *Paquita* and the *Sylvia Pas de Deux.* In addition, it offers such acknowledged modern classics as Fokine's *Scheherazade,* Nijinska's *Les Biches,* Lichine's *Graduation Ball,* Ruth Page and Bentley Stone's *Frankie and Johnny,* Agnes de Mille's *Fall River Legend,* Valerie Bettis's *A Streetcar Named Desire,* John Taras's *The Firebird,* and Frederic Franklin's *A Creole Giselle.* In the works of choreographer Geoffrey Holder (*Banda* and *Bele*), classically trained dancers are transformed into arresting interpreters of the ethnic style. In all, the DTH is a company that, like its major counterparts, presents a distinguished repertory mounted with meticulous authenticity of style but with an extra sense of originality in terms of dramatic interpretation, costuming, and decor.

The rise of DTH is, in a way, closely aligned to Mitchell's own professional rise some 20 years earlier, for his was an achievement born of struggle and determination—of grasping opportunities and turning them into positive action.

Born in New York City on March 27, 1934, Arthur Mitchell, the son of a building superintendent, grew up in Harlem and, as he puts it, turned streetwise at an early age. Headstrong and fiercely independent, he was intent on making something of himself. If he knew nothing of the arts, his love of dancing was an irrepressible part of him, and doing the lindy or the jitterbug came naturally to the increasingly good-looking youngster. Seeing him dance at a junior high school party, a guidance teacher suggested he audition for the High School of Performing Arts in midtown Manhattan.

"I must have been 14 or 15, and this teacher was very encouraging. Well, I decided to take on the challenge and prepared a tap routine for the audition. When I got there, the panel of judges included Martha Graham, Lincoln Kirstein, and John Martin who was then the dance critic of the *New York Times*—names I'd never heard before. I peeked through the door and saw these very well-trained dancers auditioning—and I was taken aback. But I went out and did my thing, and I was accepted into the school. During that first year, I was a renegade ... I couldn't follow orders, because I had been put into a structured situation that I didn't understand. I was in a middle-class world, and it was alien to me. On top of that, I knew I had a difficult body. My feet weren't very good. I didn't have a good turnout. My shoulders weren't very wide. Just about everything seemed to be wrong. Finally, I was told that I would probably never be a dancer."

Mitchell, stubborn to the end, thought otherwise. He applied himself with renewed vigor to the demands of intensive training and, upon graduation, emerged as the only male student to receive the High School of Performing Arts Dance Award. This award brought with it a scholarship to the School of American Ballet, the official school of the New York City Ballet. He also won a scholarship to Bennington College.

"I finally settled on going to Balanchine's School of American Ballet, because I felt that if I had the training in classical dance, along with the modern, tap, jazz, and ethnic that I had already studied, then no matter what I'd be asked to dance, I'd be able to do it."

Following 4 years of study at the School of American Ballet, as well as brief appearances with the companies of Donald McKayle and John Butler, Mitchell was invited to join the New York City Ballet—the first black dancer ever to appear with the company. At 22, he possessed a charismatic presence and readily proved himself equal to the Balanchine esthetic of athleticism, speed, and musicality. After a few years of dancing in the corps de ballet, he was promoted to soloist and, soon thereafter, to principal dancer. He performed major roles in the company's vast repertory, standing out in such Balanchine works as *Agon, Western Symphony,* and *A Midsummer Night's Dream* and in

Jerome Robbins's *Afternoon of a Faun.* Partnering many of the company's ballerinas, he proved a great favorite with audiences and critics alike. As for being the company's sole black dancer, Mitchell claims that during his 15 years with the City Ballet, he had never been made to feel uncomfortable or "different."

However, George Balanchine has said that when he hired Arthur Mitchell, he encountered considerable criticism.

"People objected," Mr. Balanchine said. "They told me, 'What are you going to do with him? He's black!' I said, 'He will dance.' Finally, Arthur became integrated, not in a black sense, but in a *whole* sense. I never gave him a role because of his color, only because he could dance it. You must understand that Negro blood or Japanese blood or Russian blood doesn't mean a thing to me. I don't take people because they are black or white. I take exquisite people—people who are *made* to dance. If I saw a black dancer who was only adequate, I would not take him. Should I hire a black dancer just because he is black? No! It's not right. Because I take only the best. I cannot accommodate dancers just because they are black. My life is about deciding who is worthy or good enough to be a first dancer. When I took Arthur, it was because in my eyes he *was* good enough and worthy. When Arthur started his own company, I helped him in every way I could—I helped him even before the foundations came along with grants. Anyway, Arthur took a big gamble, and I'm sure he will succeed."

If DTH was a gamble, Arthur Mitchell prepared himself in ways that would make the gamble pay off. Not only did he enlist the help of Balanchine, who gave ample advice and allowed him to perform many of his works free of charge, but he schooled himself in the nitty gritty of business procedures.

"I immersed myself in making the company a self-sustaining organization. I contacted friends in every area—lawyers, accountants, Wall Street people—and garnered tremendous expertise. I formed a board of directors, and we solicited grants and private funds. I sat down and studied all the other major ballet companies to see what their problems were—and I tried to circumvent them. In a way, I exploded the myth that artists were not good business people. And so, little by little, I shaped the company. Actually, I didn't start out wanting a company—I wanted a school first. but I needed my school kids to see the fruition of what they were studying, something to aim for and look up to. Now, students in the school are fed into the company—and that's the lifeblood of any ballet company. I might add that our school is supported entirely by our company. Usually, it's the school's income that helps support a company."

Almost since its inception, DTH has made elaborate tours both here and abroad. The company has traveled to Europe, Israel, Japan, and Australia garnering extraordinary praise. The company was honored in 1988 by an invitation to perform in the Soviet Union. Audiences the world over have been deeply impressed by the company's high standards and have taken particular note of its roster of superb principal dancers—Virginia Johnson, Lowell Smith, Donald Williams, Stephanie Dabney, Lorraine Graves, and Eddie Shellman—dancers whose technical mastery matches that of the world's major ballet stars. Indeed, DTH has spawned young artists who have been invited to join the ranks of other important companies.

Arthur Mitchell's ultimate hope for his company is to see it racially integrated—an instrument that exists purely in celebration of dance.

"You can't go on beating a dead horse," he said. "We've proven that blacks can do classical dance. Now I want a company with two of every race in the world and put them on stage and have them all dancing—a kind of Noah's ark! It won't matter who, why, or where they came from—only that they're wonderful artists. I mean, dancing is dancing! And I feel that dance is the mother of all the arts. Before a child is even out of the womb, it kicks—and kicking is dancing. The state that the world is in today, and all the preaching that's going on, makes movement take on a different value. The esthetics of dance— the beauty of it, the line of it, the physicality of it—that's communication . . . that's freedom!"

Murray Louis

Photograph by Max Waldman

Murray Louis

To watch the work of Murray Louis is to be in contact with a sensibility that makes of dance a statement not of fiction but of poetry. Like a poet, Louis deals with essence, suggestions, innuendo, and abstraction. The vocabulary of his movements is drenched in the serendipitous continuity produced by instinct, rather than by rigid forethought or design. It is choreography guided by the unexpected and fortuitous moment, choreography that instantly yields the propelling thrust for what comes next. Therefore, the gestures and movements found in a Murray Louis ballet tend to look poetically isolated, disconnected, abrupt, and quirky. At the same time, Louis's handling of space has the delicacy of forms in nature unfolding in slow-motion, like flora undulating gently underwater.

In the last several years, the Murray Louis Dance Company has moved into the vanguard of modern dance groups. The public, particularly the young, are responding more fully to the hypnotic and awkward beauty of Louis's work. They are drawn to the clarity, terseness, and deceptive simplicity of a style that, despite its individuality, emerged out of the lessons of the late German Expressionist choreographer Mary Wigman (1886–1973)—whose tense, introspective, and somber vision of dance has influenced any number of modern choreographers—and out of the work of Hanya Holm (b. 1893), Wigman's foremost pupil, who disseminated these lessons in America.

A more immediate factor in Murray Louis's creative development is his long and ongoing association with Alwin Nikolais—an early pupil of Hanya Holm—in whose company Louis danced for many years before turning to choreography and forming his own company in 1953. Murray Louis's style differs dramatically from Nikolais's unique and starkly dehumanized approach to dance, in which electronic music, lighting, and slide-projections are all composed and created by Nikolais himself. Louis allows only some of these elements to enter his choreography. In *Geometrics* (1974), for example, the electronic score, as well as the lighting, was composed by Nikolais. But, save for these occasional collaborations, the Murray Louis Dance Company bears no stylistic resemblance to the Nikolais Dance Theatre, nor, indeed, to any other contemporary modern dance group.

A tall, dark, intense man and a performer whom Clive Barnes has described as a "virtuoso dancer with a kind of muscular control that probably cannot be matched," Murray Louis is felicitously verbal about his background and about the meaning and content of his work.

"I am a New Yorker, and as a teenager I was very fortunate to be able to see a great many of the early modern dance groups," Louis says. "I saw Graham, Humphrey, Weidman, and Tamiris when I was about 13-years-old. Oddly enough, I was never really attracted to modern dance, because it was so strongly dominated by very strong and intense women. They always dressed so severely and were always deeply, deeply serious—at least, that was my impression as a wide-eyed youngster. But along with all that starkness and gloom, I fell under the spell of Fred Astaire, whose dancing in films I studied very carefully. So, I have this early mixture of female intensity and Fred Astaire!

"I always liked to dance. In fact, I felt I was a born dancer. In time, I met Alwin Nikolais, who had just begun teaching at the Henry Street Playhouse in New York, and I began to study with him there. I had all my initial training with Nikolais. Later, we became colleagues. I danced in his company and began to choreograph. At that time, we shared dancers, who would perform a season of Nikolais works and a season of my works. Then, in 1968, I formed my own group with my own dancers."

While Louis no longer dances with the Nikolais company, he continues to dance with his eight-member troupe—and to stunning effect. Speaking about his work, Louis readily admits that he is an eclectic choreographer:

"I don't operate out of one stylistic premise. I enjoy the great variety of my thematic statements. I believe strongly that the word 'performance' is the culmination of the skill of the artist-performer and the skill of the artist-choreographer uniting with those latent skills of artistry that rest in the viewer. When I compose my dances, I think of using my materials in such a manner that will awaken within the audience the same thread, the same track, the same response factors that both the performers and the choreographer uses, so that the thing becomes a unit."

Louis considers his work as a triumvirate, in which the choreographer, the dancer, and the audience form an essential totality. He accomplishes this by working within a framework of abstraction—of abstract movement, which is neither specific nor literal, but which allows an audience to bring its own imagination to bear upon any given work.

"The thing that is essential to the way I work is that *what* I do rests within the movement. I really don't tell stories, although sometimes things look almost pantomimic, and that is because the movement, abstract as it is, is so clear. You can read it. Basically, I work out of evolution. That is, when a dance suggests itself, and I find that I know where I'm going with it, I let it evolve out of its own nature. I make coherences out of movement relationships. And I let the piece go where it wants to go. I guide the dance very strongly, but I guide it out of an intuitive vision. I do not intrude on a piece. There is a difference between intrusion and guidance. When an artist intrudes, he is coercing the innate nature of a particular work. When he guides, he allows the piece to *occur.* Often, I can hardly wait to see in which direction a piece is going. I hope it is as intriguing for the audience as it is for me."

Since its inception, the Murray Louis Dance Company has toured widely, often under government sponsorship. The company has performed regularly throughout the United States, as well as in 20 countries on four continents—Louis has created new works for the Berlin State Opera Company, the Scottish Ballet, and the Royal Danish Ballet. He also made a five-part film series, *Dance as an Art Form,* and choreographed *By George,* a piece with music by George Gershwin, for the Cleveland Ballet. In the past few years, he has created several new dances for his own company, including *Four Brubeck Pieces, Act One* (both performed in live concert with the Dave Brubeck Quartet), *Revels,* and *The Disenchantment of Pierrot.* In June of 1984, Louis was made "Knight of the Order of Arts and Letters" in Paris.

Clearly, Murray Louis and the Murray Louis Dance Company have achieved international stature—a fact that readily qualifies them as a national treasure.

Antony Tudor

Photograph by Nina Alovert

Antony Tudor

It had been 7 years since Antony Tudor had created a new ballet. This long choreographic silence by one of the world's most important and enigmatic choreographers was broken in 1975 when American Ballet Theatre (ABT)—of which Tudor was Associate Director—presented *The Leaves Are Fading*, a 30-minute work set to music by Anton Dvořák.

In ballet circles, a new Tudor work constituted a major event. Having created such acknowledged masterpieces as *Pillar of Fire, Jardin aux lilas, Romeo and Juliet, Dark Elegies, Dim Lustre*, and *Undertow*, the London-born choreographer brought a unique vocabulary to dance, one that subtly combined elements of classical and modern techniques, while laying bare the psychological underpinnings of his characters.

In a Tudor ballet, the most infinitesimal gesture holds meaning. Every action, every stance, every movement contains a true link with feeling and emotion. Tudor's characters are rooted in life, and their emotions develop out of life's problems. Tudor was a master of nuance. The most fleeting glance, the most casual touch of the hand, revealed an inner life. Indeed, if there is an underlying and unifying motif in Tudor's oeuvre, it is the crystallization of human expression—the finding of heightened emotions through the economy and understatement of stylized movements.

One felt slightly apprehensive in the presence of Antony Tudor. A tall man, with piercing eyes and a bald head, he conveyed an image of birdlike alertness. Nothing seemed to escape his gaze. A diffident man, he was not given to light or casual banter. Interviews were particularly anathema to Tudor, and it was with greatest reluctance that, in 1975, he agreed to discuss *The Leaves Are Fading*, as well as his long absence from the choreographic scene.

"I don't really want to talk about my new ballet, mainly because it's driving me out of my mind," he said. "The trouble is, I can't move. I can't move at all. You see, my body is much older. When I choreograph, I like to show every movement that everyone does. I have to feel everything through my own body, always. I *have* to do my ballets like that, and I'm finding it very, very hard. I've got two poor, long-suffering dancers with whom I'll be meeting in a little while, and I don't know if I can make up a movement. Perhaps in 3 years I'll have a ballet! The fact is, I feel I've been cornered into doing this work. People are mad to expect anything at all!"

During the months that Tudor worked on *The Leaves Are Fading,* he permitted no visitors into the studio. Only bits and pieces of information trickled out: The work would not have a specific story, it would be Tudor's first abstract ballet—a string of unrelated dances. Rudolf Nureyev, Natalia Makarova, or Mikhail Baryshnikov, all clamoring for a new Tudor work to be created on them, would *not* be in it. ("They will have to wait!" Tudor said.) Instead, the ballet would feature Gelsey Kirkland and Jonas Kage. There would be sets and costumes by Ming Cho Lee. The Dvořák music would be drawn from the composer's chamber works.

Tudor admitted that his new ballet would, indeed, be his first major abstract work: "Well, yes. It's a piece without any story at all—which other people do so brilliantly. Of course, if I see a human body on the stage, I don't see it as an abstraction. I see it as a body. So, I would not call this new work of mine 'abstract.' Rather, I'd call it 'empty,' which, though a dangerous word, isn't quite the same as 'abstract.'

"I'm foolhardy to have attempted it at all. I didn't want to open it in New York. I wanted to open it in some little town in Oregon. The whole thing is a madness! Anyway, why put myself at the mercy of the great American public in order to commit suicide—in order to hear people say, 'Tudor isn't what we thought he was!' You know, last year, ABT had an all-Tudor evening. As I left the theater, I overheard someone saying, 'Three Tudor ballets in one evening! That's a bit much, isn't it?' I agreed wholeheartedly. Oh, I suppose some of the movements in the new ballet will have some people sighing with pleasure—especially the old-timers. But that doesn't mean that the people next to them won't be fast asleep and snoring."

What had taken Antony Tudor so long to create a new ballet?

"I've said this again and again! I don't like to work! No one will believe me! I mean, you start getting an idea for a ballet, and you're up against all that nonsense of devising steps and going through that whole torture again. Because it *is* torture for the choreographer as well as for the dancer. You can go for 3 days knowing there's a movement you want, and you can't find it.

"Also, I never wanted to repeat myself. Once I had done *Undertow,* in 1945, I had come to the end of my so-called psychological ballets. *Undertow* is the study of a murderer. Well I wasn't interested in that anymore, so I moved on to *The Echoing of Trumpets* (1963), which was quite a change of pace for me. It was a work that more or less dealt with political upheaval. Then, I did *Shadowplay* (1967), which, again, was different from anything I'd done before. It was slightly philosophical in background. Then, I decided to do a real Restoration-type comedy, because I hadn't touched a comedy for a great many years. That was *Knight Errant,* which I set on the touring section of London's Royal Ballet in 1968. Then, I simply stopped. I had run out of subjects that interested me, and I could never find an appropriate score. It was as simple as that. Besides, there were a good many young choreographers around who were doing rather interesting things. I thought it would be nice for them to have the field to themselves."

During Tudor's self-imposed creative silence, he did not, however, remain idle. He traveled throughout the world, staging his ballets for various major companies. Having developed an intense interest in Zen Buddhism, he devoted himself more fully to its study and practice. In 1974, he was persuaded by Lucia Chase and Oliver Smith to joint ABT as Associate Director, a post that required him to take an active part in the company's artistic policies. In point of fact, Tudor's association with ABT began in 1940 when the company was first formed. He had been invited to come from England to stage some of his ballets and to create new ones. Tudor created *Pillar of Fire* (1942), *Romeo and Juliet* (1943), *Dim Lustre* (1943), and *Shadow of the Wind* (1948) for ABT. To this day, ABT remains the largest repository of Tudor's work, and the company has never failed to present a Tudor ballet during each of its seasons.

It has been said that Tudor changed the lives of the dancers he worked with. A case in point was the late American ballerina Nora Kaye, for whom Tudor created *Pillar of Fire* in 1942. Miss Kaye emerged a star under Tudor's demanding tutelage and guidance—a guidance noted for its obsessive and almost tyrannical insistence on creative meticulousness. It is well known in the ballet world that the physical and psychological pressures put on Nora Kaye would have broken the spirit of a less tenacious or less dedicated artist. Sallie Wilson, a principal dancer with ABT until 1980, and one of the foremost interpreters of the Tudor repertory, had fallen helplessly under the spell of Tudor—the man, as well as his work. "I survived Tudor by myself," she has said. "He didn't help me to survive at all. If I were a different person, I would not be dancing today." Cynthia Gregory, an equally brilliant Tudor dancer, recalled her first encounter with the choreographer: "When I first came to ABT, Tudor was reviving *Pillar of Fire.* I was one of the Sexy Girls in it. I was scared to death of Tudor. He was kind of a scary person. I would work with him, and he would humiliate me. I would cry. It was difficult. Things became easier later in his life—he mellowed. But Tudor liked to sort of torture you. He would look at you and immediately know your weak spots. He had such uncanny perception about people!"

From Tudor's point of view, dancers are creatures full of false illusions about themselves.

"What you must do with dancers is to strip them of their superficialities—strip them of their own conception of themselves, until you find something underneath. They say I make them cry. Well, they make me cry too. It's not a one-way street. You see, the whole of art is generally considered as an economy. I mean, an El Greco economy isn't the same as a Tang Dynasty Chinese painter's economy. It must be limited to exactly what is wanted. There must be no excrescences. So many dancers *like* their excrescences. And their excrescences work extremely well with the public. I don't like them at all, however. When I work with a dancer, I like to get to the core, because ... what is in the core? The seed. And what is in the seed? The future!"

With some prodding, Tudor did reveal a bit more about *The Leaves Are Fading*. Did the title of the ballet have any special significance?

"No, no special significance. People can make of it what they will. In the meantime, it's a horror to work on. I just threw out 5 minutes of it. It was a section I loved, but I couldn't work with it. I thought I could do it, but it turned out to be better than me. It won! It developed its own immortality, and so, I had to throw it out. I had a group of girls, and I worked out a lot of movements on them. And it was all quite beautiful. Then, it began to bore me, and I felt it would bore the audience. If you sense that you're sending the audience very quietly and pleasantly to sleep, then I think you should try to avoid that.

"What else? Well, I'm having a terrible time with the music. I'm using sections of Dvořák's *The Cypresses,* his String Quintet Opus 77, the String Quartet Opus 80, and parts of his *Terzetto.* It's incredibly hard to make those pieces fit together, because of the changes in tonality from key to key. Dvořák composed in too many of the wrong keys! So, all of that has become very difficult."

What of his involvement with Zen?

"I've not been involved lately, because I've been traveling a good deal. Then, some weeks ago, I injured my knee which makes it very difficult to sit cross-legged. Naturally, it's part of me. I couldn't get rid of this particular attachment. Of course, the longer you're with Zen, the less you know about it—thank God! And you get no results from it. It's very tough, very challenging.

"Now, I think I've talked quite enough," said Tudor, rising. "I've got to go back into that studio and see if I can still put movements together. This whole business has been a journey of horrifying discovery for me. I can't imagine why I ever got back into it again!"

Antony Tudor died in April of 1987 at the age of 79. The last decade of his life was one of many achievements. Although he had ceased choreographing, his works were performed throughout the world. In 1980, he was given the title Choreographer Emeritus by ABT; in this capacity, he oversaw the revivals of several of his ballets, including *Pillar of Fire* (performed in 1982 and 1987). Numerous awards came his way. In 1986, he received both the Capezio Award, which he had modestly refused to accept a few years earlier, and the Kennedy Center Honors, the highest recognition for an artist working in the US. Agnes de Mille summed up Tudor's achievements in her remarks at the Kennedy Center ceremony:

Antony was a strong classicist, that is, he revered form. He wanted to find fine patterns for himself, beautiful patterns, beautiful gestures, but they must be new, not shopworn, surprising, not only new but clear, instantly recognizable for what they meant, moving. In short, magic.

John Taras

Photograph courtesy of American Ballet Theatre

John Taras

When John Taras was appointed Associate Director of American Ballet Theatre (ABT) in July of 1984, the career of this greatly beloved figure in the dance world—a man linked professionally with the New York City Ballet (NYCB) for a quarter of a century—appeared to come full circle. It was in 1941 that a promising 22-year-old dancer was invited to join what was then called Ballet Theatre. For the next 5 years, John Taras's life became closely involved with a company that would nurture his talent, not only as a dancer, but also as a ballet-master and choreographer.

Although it came as a shock when it was announced in July of 1984 that Taras would be leaving NYCB, it was undoubtedly the death of NYCB's legendary George Balanchine in 1983 that ultimately prompted him to accept Mikhail Baryshnikov's invitation to cross over and join ABT.

A man of grace and cultivation, John Taras held the position of balletmaster at the NYCB. Perhaps the least prepossessing of the company's highly visible and powerful men behind the scenes—including Lincoln Kirstein, Jerome Robbins, and Peter Martins—Taras nevertheless wielded enormous influence in a company noted for its intense individualism and immersion in the Balanchine aesthetic. Although himself a choreographer of note (his works have long been prominently featured in the NYCB repertory), he was in many ways the true custodian of George Balanchine's ballets, the keeper of the Balanchine flame.

But with Balanchine's death, and a new administration in charge, Taras's spirits dampened. As he put it at the time, "I don't know if I really want to be around with Balanchine gone. You see, I would do anything for Mr. Balanchine, and there are very few people one can say that about. Without Balanchine, there's just no point in my staying."

When ABT's artistic director, Mikhail Baryshnikov, announced Taras's appointment, he said, "John Taras represents a combination of experience, authority, and taste which are welcomed with great enthusiasm. We all look forward to a very productive and interesting future."

There is little doubt that John Taras's future will be interesting; however, his past is positively legendary. In retrospect, it mirrors all facets of ballet history. A sweeping lesson in diversity, Taras's background offers an image of ballet at its most adventurous, chaotic, courageous, and utterly fulfilling. It is also the story of one man's search for personal and creative growth: the story of a visionary youngster who emerged a much loved, much admired, and highly respected man of dance.

John Taras, born of Ukrainian parents on April 18, 1919, starts life on New York City's Lower East Side, residing first on Sixth, then on Seventh Street, near Tompkins Square. He will live there, off and on, until the age of 21.

"I was an only child. My earliest memories center on being in and out of the Ukrainian church on East Seventh Street. My father was a cook. My mother was at home, but, unhappily, died when I was 9. After that, my father had difficulty taking care of me. I remember spending a lot of time with our janitor, an Irish woman, who taught me how to waltz to a wind-up phonograph. Later, my father sent me to the Ukrainian Folk Dance School, which was very good for me, because it kept me out of mischief.

"I had an older cousin who lived in the same tenement that we did. He was going to New York University (NYU). One day, he asked me if I'd like to come over to NYU because they were putting on a production of *A Midsummer Night's Dream,* and they needed an Indian Boy. I said, 'Sure!' So I joined this NYU theatrical company called the Washington Square Players, run by Randolph Sommerville. When I graduated from high school, I immediately enrolled at NYU and continued working with the university theater, performing every kind of role, from juveniles to princes. Finally, I did Oberon and played Marchbanks in Shaw's *Candida.* The fact is, I started out as an actor. The company was very active. We traveled to Cooperstown, NY every summer, and we performed and made our own scenery and costumes. The only thing the company *didn't* have was a choreographer—and that interested me."

At 17, John Taras becomes more and more intrigued with dance. The actress Margaret Wycherly gives him Romola Nijinsky's biography of her famous husband. In it, he reads of the Ballets Russes, about Diaghilev and his first great choreographer, Michel Fokine. As chance would have it, he discovers an advertisement in the *New York Times,* announcing that Fokine himself was now living in New York and giving ballet lessons on Riverside Drive. Losing no time, Taras presents himself at Fokine's.

"I went there in all innocence. I knew nothing. I had never taken a ballet class in my life, and I was already 17! Well, Fokine's son Vitale handled the new people, and he gave us a barre up on the fourth floor of the mansion. I'll never forget that first lesson! I could barely move, but Vitale said, 'Just follow as best as you can.' After the barre, we all went down to the salon, and there was Fokine himself, sitting at the piano teaching variations from his own ballets. On that first day, I learned the movements of the Odalisques from his *Scheherazade*. For me, that was *it!* I mean, I couldn't do anything, but it was absolutely thrilling just to go through the motions. Little by little, I managed to learn all the variations from *Carnaval, Cleopatre, Spectre de la Rose,* and *Les Sylphides.* We did them over and over again, and I came to know every last step. Of course, all of that went more into my head than into my body, because I still could hardly move. But I worked as hard as I could, even though after a couple of years I *still* couldn't dance properly. You see, I never had the basics.

"By now, it was 1938, and I continued working with the Washington Square Players at NYU and also took ballet classes with Fokine, which, I might add, were quite expensive. Anyway, that summer, the Washington Square Players didn't go to Cooperstown, but to Hofstra College in Hempstead, Long Island. It was a residency, and the company members both performed and taught acting classes. Hofstra wanted to include a dance course. Our director, Randolph Sommerville, asked if I would teach it. So, I sort of taught Morris dances and also taught a children's class."

It is at Hofstra, in the summer of 1938, that John Taras's life takes an unexpected turn. Two little girls, the daughters of Joseph and Jennie Hirshhorn, enroll in his children's dancing class. Their mother sits and observes how well the 18-year-old teacher teaches the children and how quickly and easily they respond to his lessons.

"Mrs. Hirshhorn became very interested in me. One day, she asked me to have lunch with her. At lunch she asked, 'What are you planning to do with your life?' I told her about wanting to become a dancer, but that I would really have to give it up, because my father couldn't really afford to pay for my lessons. She said, 'What would it entail for you to really get a proper education?' Brashly I answered, 'I really have to have private dancing lessons in order to catch up with what I don't know. Obviously, I have to take a class every day and a private lesson three or four times every week. Also, I really should study music and, of course, I have to have money to live on.'

"Well, it turned out that this woman was Jennie Hirshhorn, married to Joseph Hirshhorn, known as the Uranium King, a multi-millionaire whose famous art collection is now housed in the Hirshhorn Museum in Washington, DC. Anyway, she talked all this over with my teacher, Randolph Sommerville. The two made up a sort of budget of what everything would cost. A short time later, Mrs. Hirshhorn told me that she and her husband would underwrite all my studies and living expenses for the next 3 years! It was then that I *really* had to make up my mind about what I wanted to do with my life.

"Of course, at this point, all I wanted to do was dance. And I plunged into study. I had heard of a very good teacher, Madame Elisabeth Anderson-Ivantzova (1893–1973), who had studied at the Moscow Imperial School of Ballet, and had once been a ballerina with the Bolshoi. Many of my friends went to her, taking classes at her small studio on 56th Street in New York. Well, she took me and gave me private lessons and showed me everything from the very beginning, including turnout, which Fokine hated! I practically lived in her studio. We had *adagio* lessons, we had character lessons—everything. I was now 18, still living with my father part of the time and with Sommerville the rest of the time. I was also still connected with the Washington Square Players. I created the dances for their plays and still appeared in them as an actor."

The 3 years of study under the aegis of the Hirshhorns comes to an end, and John Taras, at 21, obtains his first job as a professional dancer. It is 1940, the year Taras's father dies. The young dancer is on his own, and his career in dance begins to take wing.

"My father was a marvelous man, but he never really taught me anything. He never understood what I wanted to do or, indeed, what I was doing. On his deathbed, he said, 'What are you going to do without me?' Well, he died on the day I went to an audition for my first professional job as a dancer; I got paid more in 1 week than he was ever paid in his life! It was tragic for me not to be able to prove to him that I was right in continuing with what I was doing. I got this job dancing at the New York World's Fair in a ballet created by William Dollar called *A Thousand Times Neigh!* This was a ballet spectacle held at the Ford Motor Pavilion, and the dancers in it were from George Balanchine and Lincoln Kirstein's Ballet Caravan and the American Ballet. We gave six performances a day, 7 days a week for 6 months! So, that was my very first contact with Balanchine, and I began taking classes at his School of American Ballet and got to know some of his dancers, including Nicholas Magallanes and Todd Bolender.

"When the World's Fair stint was over, I auditioned for Catherine Littlefield and her Philadelphia Ballet and was hired. Also in the company were Magallanes and Bolender, who had been with Balanchine's Ballet Caravan. We did a tour with Littlefield, and I also did a show with her called *A Kiss for Cinderella*. Then, in 1941, Magallanes, Bolender, and I joined the American Ballet Caravan, which was the new name of Balanchine's company—and that's how I met Mr. Balanchine personally.

"I watched him choreograph *Concerto Barocco*. In fact, I was the one who controlled the phonograph; I put the needle on the record. It was the time of 78 rpm records, and I'd turn the records over very quickly so as not to lose the beat and continuity of the music. So, I was in the company and appeared in the corps of everything—*Juke Box, The Bat, Billy the Kid, Ballet Imperial, Errante,* among others. Of course, Balanchine was around constantly, but I didn't pay too much attention to his presence, because I was busy learning so much. But I got to know him better when the company made its government-sponsored tour of South America in 1941, which was coordinated by Nelson Rockefeller. There were 60 dancers in the company, including Marie-Jeanne, Gisella Caccialanza, Fred Danieli, Beatrice Tompkins, Lew Christensen, John Kriza, Bolender, Magallanes, Zachary Solov, and myself. Lincoln Kirstein and his wife, Fidelma, were along and, of course, Mr. Balanchine.

"We faced incredible hardships, but we danced everywhere for 5 long months—in Brazil, Argentina, Uruguay, Chile, Peru, Colombia, and Venezuela. I remember leaving Sao Paolo and arriving in Buenos Aires. We had taken a boat called El Cabo de Buenos Esperanze. It was just at the time of the exodus of Jews caused by the German invasion of France. The boat was filled with those poor people who had escaped through the Canary Islands and through Portugal and had paid a fortune to get passage. There were 1,000 people over capacity, and the boat was absolutely filthy—just awful! In the meantime, some law had been passed in South America to the effect that girls who were minors were not allowed to work there, and some of our girls, including Marie-Jeanne, were put in jail. We had to go to the American Embassy in Buenos Aires to get them out.

"Anyway, we finished dancing in Mendoza, Argentina, and were to go on to Santiago in Chile. Well, there was an avalanche, and we were told we couldn't take a train for 6 months! Finally, army planes took us across the Andes; it was my first flight ever. It was terrifying, because the planes weren't pressurized. So we landed in Santiago, where we gave performances. Then, we took a boat from Chile to Peru—a cattleboat that stopped every day in a different port along the coast. It took us 10 days to get to where we were going. The food was inedible, but Mr. Balanchine was marvelous, because he found a way of making crepes with lime and sugar, and that's what we ate every single day. Our next stop was to be Ecuador, but we learned there was a revolution there, so we couldn't go. Instead, we went to Colombia, and then across to Venezuela, which was a 5-day automobile trip through thick jungle and terrible mountains. It was hair-raising! When we finally got to Caracas, the money had run out. Mr. Rockefeller had miscalculated the cost of the tour, and we had to come home. In all, it was an unbelievable experience. How we survived, I'll never know!"

Upon its return from South America, the American Ballet disbands. Balanchine, then married to Vera Zorina, goes to work in Hollywood. John Taras, out of a job, continues his ballet training, taking classes at the School of American Ballet and with Anatole Vilzak. He soon befriends members of Ballet Theatre, then under the artistic direction of German Sevastianov. He learns that the company would soon make a tour of Mexico and seeks to join its ranks. He is offered passage to Mexico, but is not officially hired as a dancer. Taras, now 22, accepts this condition, feeling that to have a foot in the door might mean eventual entry into Ballet Theatre.

"Ballet Theatre couldn't afford to pay me a salary, but they did pay my way to Mexico. When extra people were needed on stage, they used me. I was part of it all, which was just fine with me. I did all sorts of things, including the cooking. Alicia Markova and I would shop, peel potatoes, and scrape carrots together. I'd cook, and everyone would come to dinner—Sevastianov, Irina Baronova, Lucia Chase, Antony Tudor, Harold Lang, Markova, Anton Dolin, and Nora Kaye. Léonide Massine was with us, staging his *Aleko* and *Don Domingo,* and my old teacher, Fokine, was there doing his *Helen of Troy.* It was fabulous to be among all those incredible people.

"When we returned from Mexico, I was hired by Ballet Theatre as a corps dancer, and I stayed from 1942 to 1946. I learned all the repertoire and was in on everybody's rehearsals. I was very attentive and interested in what people were doing. I watched everything and found I had a very retentive memory. I never left the studio; I was fascinated by it all. Because of the war, we kept losing more and more men. One of them was Yurek Lazowski, our balletmaster. So, I danced in the corps of everything and became very familiar with the repertoire.

"When David Lichine staged his *Graduation Ball,* I came to know it backwards and forwards, because I danced the General in it and lots of other roles during rehearsals. Well, when Lichine left, he told Lucia

Chase that he wanted *me* to rehearse *Graduation Ball*—and that was my very first balletmaster experience. Then, when Bronislava Nijinska staged her *Harvest Time* for Tamara Toumanova and John Kriza, she asked me to take care of that. Agnes de Mille came to do *Tally Ho!*, and she asked me to rehearse it after she left. When Tudor left the company, he asked Lucia to put me in charge of *his* repertoire. Well, I not only did that, but danced all of Tudor's own roles as well. So, I really grew with the company and eventually became a soloist.

"During the '40s, Ballet Theatre was incredibly active and incredibly creative. There were all those one-night stands, and people were very close to one another. It was like a family. There was Lucia Chase, who always wanted to be treated like of one of the girls, although she was paying for absolutely everything. Annabelle Lyon was there, and Adolf Bolm came for a while as balletmaster. Of course, Jerry Robbins was around in those days, and he was a great cut-up. He'd play the piano and make fun of all the ballerinas. I remember Mme. Nijinska being furious with him most of the time, screaming at him in her fractured English. For a while, I roomed with him. That was fine, except that he'd wake up in the morning and tell me everything he'd dreamed about. I finally couldn't face that and had to change roommates. But we were always very friendly—and still are. Of course, he created *Fancy Free* for Ballet Theatre in 1944, which premiered at the Met on my birthday, April 18! I was in on the first rehearsals of that, but then Jerry decided to use John Kriza, Harold Lang, and himself in it. I almost got to do the Bartender, but the role went to Rex Cooper. Well, the ballet was an enormous success. It was Jerry's first!

"In the previous year, 1943, Vera Zorina came to perform with Ballet Theatre. Sol Hurok was presenting us at the Met, and he wanted her after Irina Baronova left. Of course, Balanchine, who was still her husband, came to help and to prepare her for *Apollo* and *Errante*. She also danced in *Helen of Troy*. I became quite friendly with Brigitta, as she was called, and Balanchine was around a great deal. Naturally, I observed him at work and he was amazing—quick, unruffled, terrifically concentrated. He adored Brigitta and coached her with tremendous care."

In the summer of 1945, John Taras, at the suggestion of Sol Hurok, stages the dances for productions of *The Merry Widow* and *The Student Prince*, being performed by a Canadian company in Toronto.

"I remained in Toronto for 10 weeks. During that time I began listening to Mozart's *Violin Concerto no. 3*, and began choreographing its second movement on Diana Adams and myself. When we got back to New York, Ballet Theatre was going into rehearsal for its fall season. It seems that Nora Kaye had gotten wind of my first choreographic effort and had told Lucia Chase about it. Well, Lucia asked to see what I had done. Afterwards, she said, 'Let's try it for the company.' So, I did the *entire* concerto in a matter of 20 hours. I used Nora Kaye, Alicia Alonso, and André Eglevsky in the first movement, Diana Adams and Richard Beard in the second, and everyone in the third. I called the ballet *Graziana.* I wanted to make a statement. I wanted it to be a purely classical work because, at the time, everyone was being an American or a cowboy, or very jazzy. The critics liked it, saying that it was good to have a nice classical ballet around.

"My second ballet was commissioned by Ballet Associates for the Original Ballet Russe. It was *Camille,* which I made for Alicia Markova and Anton Dolin. The music was Schubert arranged by Vittorio Rieti. The costumes were by Cecil Beaton. The critics didn't care for it, and I must say, I didn't think much of it either, although Markova and Dolin were lovely in it. My next work came in 1947, soon after I left Ballet Theatre. You see, I was invited to join Ballet Society, which Lincoln Kirstein and George Balanchine had formed in 1946. I danced in Balanchine's *Renard* to the Stravinsky score and choreographed a ballet called *The Minotaur* to music by Elliott Carter, with costumes and scenery by the Spanish designer, Joan Junyer. For the role of Ariadne, I took a little girl from the School of American Ballet—Tanaquil Le-Clerq, who that year had won the Ballet Society Fellowship Award. She was extraordinary! Elise Reiman and Francisco Moncion were also in the cast. Actually, *The Minotaur* was to have been choreographed by Balanchine, but he had to go the Paris Opéra as balletmaster and choreographer, and was also staging *The Chocolate Soldier* in New York. By 1947, I had become an active choreographer."

In 1945, John Taras is invited to join Colonel de Basil's Ballet Russe as dancer and balletmaster. He travels with the company on its London and Paris tours. Following a nearly fatal illness in Paris, Taras receives a sudden commission for a new ballet. The work proves a major success.

"As *regisseur* of de Basil's Ballet Russe, I rehearsed both *Les Sylphides* and *Aurora's Wedding* with Zizi Jeanmaire, who had come from the Paris Opéra under Serge Lifar. She was very much the classical dancer at the time—very good and very strong. I also danced in *Le Coq d'Or* and in Massine's *Symphonie Fantastique,* among many other ballets. When the company went to Paris, I caught meningitis. I was placed in a hospital and was in a delirium most of the time. Of course, the disease being tremendously contagious, no one came to see me. I was in agony, couldn't speak a word of French, and was absolutely miserable. I thought I would die—but I didn't. When I got out of the hospital, I was so weak that I decided I had better go back to America. I made a reservation on the Mauritania to sail back to New York. The ship would leave in 10 days.

"Well, the moment I made my reservation, I received a telegram from London, asking if I would like to stage a ballet for a new company that was being created there, called the Metropolitan Ballet. I sent back a wire saying that if I could do the ballet in 10 days, I'd come over. They agreed, and I went to London. I didn't know the company, and I didn't know what I was going to do. They suggested I do a ballet to Liszt's *Orpheus,* but I felt I couldn't do that. I suddenly thought of the music Massine had used for his *Aleko,* most of which he'd cut. It was the second movement of Tchaikovsky's *Piano Trio in A Minor.* That's what I used; I called the ballet *Designs with Strings.* I had a terrific cast: Erik Bruhn, Sonia Arova, Poul Gnatt, Celia Franca, and a girl named Delysia Blake. The scenery and costumes were by George Kirsta. The ballet premiered in Edinburgh in February, 1948, but I never saw it, because by then I had returned to America and had gone to San Francisco to mount yet another ballet of mine, *Persephone,* for the San Francisco Ballet.

"From San Francisco, I returned to New York and rejoined Ballet Society, which was repeating Balanchine's *Renard* and my own *Minotaur.* During that 1948 season, Ballet Society gave the American premiere of Balanchine's *Symphony in C,* which he had created the previous year for the Paris Opéra Ballet under the title of *Le Palais de Crystal.* Lew Christensen was to have danced in the final movement, but he injured his ankle and I was suddenly put in. I danced the fourth movement with Elise Reiman. It was the first time the ballet had been seen in New York.

"In the meantime, I had received a letter from the Metropolitan Ballet saying that *Designs with Strings* had had a great success everywhere it had gone. They invited me to go on a tour with them to Scandinavia, as dancer and choreographer. I accepted with delight, and off I went to London and finally saw my *Designs with Strings.* Then, we made a tour of Sweden and Norway. Although I did not choreograph this time around, I danced in *Les Sylphides* and in a ballet by Frank Staff called *Fanciulla,* as well as in several other works. It was not a successful tour, and eventually the company sort of collapsed. At the end of the tour, I returned to London."

While with the Metropolitan Ballet, John Taras receives a telegram from the Grand Ballet de Marquis George de Cuevas, inviting him to become its balletmaster. The year is 1949, and for the next 10 years Taras's life is closely linked with that of the erratic, unpredictable, and capricious Marquis de Cuevas.

"The Marquis was a fascinating man. He was married to Margaret Strong, a niece of John D. Rockefeller, and spent a great deal of her money in running the various ballet companies he headed, beginning in the early forties on through 1961, when he died. Actually, the company sort of hung on until 1962, and then disbanded. Well, I came to it in 1949 and had seen it perform when I was in Paris some years earlier. At the time, Rosella Hightower was its prima ballerina. I knew a lot of the dancers in the company, because many of them had been with de Basil's Ballet Russe. I agreed to become balletmaster. There was only one hitch: They hadn't informed their current balletmaster that he would be out of a job. That person was William Dollar, who was a friend of mine. Well, I wasn't going to appear on the scene until that matter had been resolved. When it finally was, I joined the company in Oxford where it was performing.

"There were all the dancers—Rosella, Marjorie Tallchief, George Skibine, André Eglevsky, and lots of corps people I knew. The repertory was a great mixture of things, and much of it was not very good. But I began to rehearse them and we went on a tour of North Africa. Then, in 1950, we came to America and presented a season on Broadway. It was a disaster. The reviews were perfectly dreadful—and with good reason. The Marquis was crestfallen, and after our Broadway run he decided to disband. Oddly enough, he announced that he would keep Rosella, André, Marjorie, George, and me on salary. Well, a dancer doesn't want to be paid and just sit at home and do nothing! So I started thinking. Since we were getting a salary, why not reorganize? We could recruit a whole new set of dancers and start fresh. The Marquis thought that was an excellent idea.

"As it turned out, the Marquis still had to fulfill a contract to give a 4-week season at the Casino in Cannes and a 4-week season in Deauville. We would organize a brand new company and have 8 weeks to work. The conditions were rather strict: If the venture didn't work, we would give up our money and disband. Well, Eglevsky thought that was too risky and he left. But the rest of us agreed to meet in Cannes and teach our repertory to a completely new set of dancers. We would do *Swan Lake*—Act II, *Giselle,* and other works, including my *Designs with Strings* and Bill Dollar's *Constanzia.* We opened in Cannes and were a huge success. We then received an engagement to perform at the Théâtre de l'Empire in Paris and, again, we were a triumph. So, our idea had worked and we got engagements all over; we supported ourselves.

"In 1952, I choreographed a ballet called *Piege de Lumière* for Rosella Hightower and Vladimir Skouratoff; it was a great success. In fact, things were going very well for me, except that the Marquis could be quite difficult and his wife, the Marchesa, was completely impossible. You see, de Cuevas was not really a professional man. He couldn't handle money, and he was continually forced to ask his wife to supply him with it. I'm afraid not all the monies meant for the ballet went to the ballet. There were a great many friends who benefited from the Marquis's friendship. They would get little presents. The Marquis kept people on salary—just on a whim. There were quite a few ladies and gentlemen who wouldn't be alive today if it weren't for him. He was very generous and very erratic. And always, he had to ask the Marchesa for money. He'd be quite outrageous about it, too, such as the time he suddenly 'fell ill' and wired her, saying, 'I'm dying! Please send $5,000!' And the money would come.

"Finally, as far as I was concerned, the difficulty was the Marchesa, *not* the Marquis. You see, in those years, I was really running the company. I was in charge, because the dancers *wanted* me in charge. Well, the Marchesa, who was never around, hadn't the vaguest idea of who I was or what I did. For her, the names were Nijinska, Lifar, or Balanchine. The designers she knew were Dali, Derain, and Goncharova. I counted for very little in her eyes, and that ultimately caused me to leave. It was my first break with the Grand Ballet, and it occurred in 1954.

"I lived in Paris, and by this time people had heard of me. I went to work for the National Ballet in Holland for a time. I staged a production of Weill's *Three-Penny Opera* in Paris. I staged ballets for opera in Aix-en-Provence—*Orpheus, Don Giovanni, Figaro, Carmen.* I staged Balanchine's *Sonnambula* and *Concerto Barocco* for the Royal Danish Ballet. I was tremendously busy. Then, 2 years later, the Marquis called me and asked me to come back. Foolishly, I did.

"There were lots of different dancers. Marjorie Tallchief and Skibine had left. There was George Zoritch, Genia Melikova, Nina Verubova, and Denise Bourgeois. I composed more ballets, one of them being *Cordelia*—with music by Sauget and decor by Jacques Dupont—danced by Zoritch and Dolores Starr, an American. I stayed until 1959 at which time I met with the same difficulties I had encountered in 1954. Again, it was the Marchesa, who felt she had to make herself known. I mean, she didn't really give a damn about me or the company, but she wanted it known that the money came from her. Well, I just sort of gave up. Besides, I had turned 40 and felt I had better get back to the States."

John Taras lives in Europe for over 10 years. He befriends the rich and famous, including Aristotle Onassis, under whose aegis he creates a ballet on the occasion of the marriage of Prince Rainier to Grace Kelly. Throughout his years abroad, he matures as a man, dancer, choreographer, and balletmaster. It is a long, fruitful, and, at times, difficult apprenticeship. It is now time to return to his roots.

"I got back to New York in the fall of 1959, and one day I went up to Broadway and 83rd Street, where Balanchine's School of American Ballet was then located. I hadn't seen Mr. B. for ages, and there he was, rehearsing for the following season. 'What are you doing here?' he asked. I told him I had decided to come back. 'And starve with the rest of us!' he added. I told him I was looking for something to do. He said, 'Why don't you stage *Sonnambula* for us?' I told him I'd be delighted. So, almost immediately, I rehearsed *Sonnambula*. Balanchine would come and watch me work. At the end of it, he asked me if I'd like to stay and work with the company. Naturally, I agreed. By now, what had been Balanchine's and Kirstein's Ballet Society had become the New York City Ballet (NYCB). The company was fairly large and was performing at the City Center.

"At the time I joined, NYCB was presenting a festival of Latin American composers, and Lew Christensen was to have choreographed something to Ginastera's *Variaziones Concertantes.* For some reason, Lew didn't do it, and Mr. B. asked if I'd like to do it, which I did. Later, they did a jazz festival based on music by classical composers. I choreographed Stravinsky's *Ebony Concerto,* which was then repeated during the Stravinsky Festival of 1972.

"When Mr. B. asked me to come to the City Ballet, back in 1959, Janet Reed was balletmistress. I was called Assistant to Mr. Balanchine. Then, when Jerry Robbins wanted to come back in the late '60s, we were all given the title of balletmaster—including Mr. B. Mr. Balanchine never wanted to be called artistic director, because he felt that the head of a company is the balletmaster. He said, 'Marius Petipa was never artistic director; he was balletmaster!' Anyway, when I got there, Maria Tallchief, Erik Bruhn, Conrad Ludlow, Jacques D'Amboise, Allegra Kent, Patricia Wilde, and the very young Patricia McBride were all dancing. The company was in very good shape, indeed, and I was delighted to be part of it."

John Taras reflects on his 20-odd years with the New York City Ballet.

"Mr. Balanchine knew what he liked. He didn't tell you what to do. On the other hand, his was the last word—including decisions on the running of the school. At times, he would be difficult. Often, I disagreed with him. But the distressing thing was, he always turned out to be right. It just took a long time for me to learn that. He had an extraordinary eye and an extraordinary way of thinking. I mean, you would say, 'My God! Why does he take *that* dancer for that part?' Then suddenly, you would realize that that person was exactly right for it. And he thought of everyone. If he'd done a ballet for, say, Suzanne Farrell, he would do one next for Patty McBride or for Merrill Ashley or someone else. What was so extraordinary about Mr. B. was that he could choreograph *anything*. He could change from one genre to another. You couldn't really ask, 'What is a Balanchine ballet?', because they're all so different.

"It's true that there weren't many outside choreographers at NYCB, but that was because Balanchine never really approved of people coming in from the outside. It was Lincoln Kirstein who pushed for other choreographers coming in and, early on, we had Tudor and Ashton and Birgit Cullberg. But Mr. B. never really liked that. I don't even know what he thought of Jerry Robbins or if he totally approved of his work. Anyway, he liked to keep it all in the family.

"The company has gotten very big—maybe too big. And the dancers have gotten somewhat lax. Today, the moment anyone has the slightest injury, they go out. If you have a small company, no one ever seems to get injured. But now, the feeling is, 'Oh, someone else can do it.' Some of our younger dancers complain that there's not enough coaching. Well, there's never been much coaching at City Ballet. You're taught the ballets and you have to run with them. Mr. Balanchine never wanted his dancers to *act* a ballet. He wanted them to do the steps, and *that* you can only do by working by yourself. Of course, a balletmaster can tell you when you're not on the music or correct this and that, but a lot of it is really your own work. People sometimes complain that the corps dancing at City Ballet is sloppy, but, you see, it was Balanchine's wish that the company *not* have the look of uniformity, like the English have. When the arms of the corps flopped around—he didn't really mind that. It's irritating to some people, but he'd say, 'Look at a garden. All the flowers are different! Look at those roses! No rose resembles another.' So, in *Serenade,* for example, if there is the sense of regimentation and uniformity, it becomes a bore. It's just a different way of thinking about dancing. Balanchine wanted a kind of freedom.

"Mr. B. and I were friends. But when we would get together privately, we never talked about ballet. We talked about wine and about truffles! We talked about vanilla beans and all the things that go into making good cooking. He had very strong likes and dislikes about food, and I always hesitated to invite him to dinner or to recommend restaurants. But I did have one triumph in France. I took him to a restaurant in Paris called Camelia. I told him they had wonderful truffles, and we went there. The first thing we ordered was a salad of truffles and he said, 'This is what I've dreamed of all my life!'

"When Mr. Balanchine died, one thought, What will happen next? How will things go on? Well, things will not be the same. It just couldn't be the same.

"What keeps me going now is the memory of George Balanchine. He is the one who has rewarded me most in the ballet world. I never had as much pleasure as I've had from his ballets . . . from watching him work, from being near him and seeing the way he was, the way he talked, the way he taught, the way he cooked—everything!"

Lucia Chase

Photograph by Martha Swope

Lucia Chase

In the world of ballet, perhaps the most private person in public life was Lucia Chase (1907–1986), former codirector of American Ballet Theatre (ABT).

"If you'll forgive me, I have always led a very double life, and I'd like to keep it that way," Miss Chase said curtly when I approached her for an interview in 1974.

But this ironclad rule was momentarily eased, when Miss Chase was assured that prying into her personal life would not be the subject of our talk—that, on the contrary, I wished only to explore her deep feelings for a company that through her tenacity, good judgment, and vision has achieved international recognition and stature. Of course, to learn something of the woman behind the visionary would help explain ABT's durability and grandeur. Miss Chase consented to see me at her luxurious duplex apartment on New York's Park Avenue.

The silent ascent in the elevator set the tone of my visit. At the appointed floor, the door was opened by an aging and cordial butler. He made me wait in an austere and silent living room. Miss Chase, I was told, would join me momentarily. I stood in a room that revealed much that was left unsaid between us. It was a somber room, though not oppressive. Superb oils of sporting scenes dominated the walls, as well as portraits by such masters as Sir Joshua Reynolds. The furniture, European and early American, suggested wealth and understated elegance. On the grand piano stood expensively framed photographs: an early wedding-portrait; two little boys seated and smiling on a rocking-horse; a ballerina in costume; the portrait of a young and radiantly beautiful woman, smiling at life. These were Miss Chase's silent and poignant reminders of a past that included memories of both joy and tragedy.

"Won't you have something to drink?" said Miss Chase, who had appeared, all smiles, wearing a simple green tailored dress. In a few moments, the butler brought a glass of scotch on a silver tray. Miss Chase and I sat on dark green divans, facing each other. An irrepressible sense of life and alertness attended this vivacious and still beautiful woman. In a way, she offered a charming contradiction to her staid and affluent surroundings. A bubbling and powerful personality continually belied the quiet of the room's muted ambiance.

Surprisingly, Miss Chase *did* reveal some facts about her private life. "I was married only once—and to a wonderful, wonderful man," she told me. "Then, after 6 years and 2 months, he suddenly died.

There was only time for two children ... our two little boys. I'd like to have had at least two more. I had no idea my husband was so very sick. He died in 1933. It was, of course, a great, great shock. I thought we were going to live together forever! And we would have! I have not remarried. I just never could. It was too perfect. And I wanted my two boys to remember their father."

Years later, a second tragedy befell Lucia Chase. Her eldest son, out sailing his boat, was caught in a storm. He was lost at sea, his body never recovered. "He was the most wonderful boy—exactly like his father," said Miss Chase with a sad smile.

It was the shock of her husband's death in 1933 that propelled Lucia Chase into nonstop creative and professional activity. But even from the first, her life was dedicated to the stage.

"From the time I was 3, I always wanted to be an actress. I always wanted the stage, and my mother and father were very good about it. So, I left Waterbury, Connecticut, where I was born, and went to New York. I studied acting at the Theatre Guild School and met lots and lots of wonderful people. Then, one day, I met Mikhail Mordkin, who, as you know, was Anna Pavlova's great partner. Well, Mordkin had opened a school in New York, and I began attending his ballet classes. In those days, I took all sorts of lessons. I took singing lessons, piano lessons, and acting lessons. I took all the lessons I could. But, after my husband died, it was really Mr. Mordkin who helped to put me back on my feet. He was wonderful. He enjoyed working with me and was an inspiration to work with."

Lucia Chase, gifted and beautiful, eventually became a ballerina with the Mordkin Ballet. During 1938 and 1939, she danced leading roles in *Giselle, La Fille Mal Gardée,* and *The Goldfish,* among others. At the time, the company included such dancers as Viola Essen, Patricia Bowman, Nina Stroganova, Leon Danielian, Leon Varkas, and Dimitri Romanoff. The company's business manager was Rudolf Orthwine, a man of enormous acumen and conviviality (he would later be founder and publisher of *Dance Magazine*), who guided the Mordkin Ballet through its initial season. Also on the scene was a young man by the name of Richard Pleasant. It was Pleasant who, in 1940, founded Ballet Theatre, later to become American Ballet Theatre.

"Richard Pleasant thought it was time for America to have its own ballet company," Miss Chase recalled. "And it was Dick who thought that such a company should *not* have a choreographer as its head, but that many choreographers should come and work with it. And so, during that first year, he invited 11 choreographers from all over the world. Each treated the company as his own. Of course, Mordkin was there, and Mikhail Fokine, Antony Tudor, Agnes de Mille, and others came along. You see, it was Richard Pleasant's great wish that Ballet Theatre would always be a gallery of the dance; that it would present all the best in ballet; that it would be a great international company but American in spirit. We have followed his vision exactly as he saw it that very first year."

Ballet Theatre's first year proved exhilarating, but, as with many young and idealistic enterprises, financially unstable.

"Dick Pleasant tried desperately to raise money so that we could keep going," Miss Chase continued. "Well, he had a terrible time of it. Finally, in 1941, he resigned as Ballet Theatre's first director and went on to other things. Then, Sol Hurok took us over, and he sent us German Sevastianov, who became our managing director. We continued under the Hurok banner until 1945. Hurok was a wonderful person, but we had many disagreements. You see, he was an impresario. At first, he would advertise us as 'S. Hurok is Proud to Present Ballet Theatre.' Then, he began advertising 'The Greatest in Russian Ballet by the Ballet Theatre.' Each year, the Russian Ballet got bigger and Ballet Theatre got smaller. When the Marquis de Cuevas started coming around, we could see that Hurok, sensing lots of money, would merge us with de Cuevas's company, or drop us, or something, and that Dick's idea of an American ballet company would go by the board. And so, in 1945, we broke with Hurok, and continued Ballet Theatre on our own."

It was at this moment that Lucia Chase was asked to become the company's new director. I asked Miss Chase how it was that she was chosen to run such a complex enterprise.

"Oh, well, I was there from the beginning. I was enthusiastic and a busybody. I was into everything. I was a happy dancer for 5 years!"

But, I ventured, did she not also aid the company financially? Did she not pour part of her own fortune into it?

"I never *poured* anything!" Miss Chase answered, clearly piqued. "I'll tell you what it was. In the beginning, when Dick Pleasant started to shape the company, he though he could get four people to give $25,000.00 each. Well, I gave that amount, but nobody knew about it. I helped Dick, but very secretly. And I hated every bit of it. I never meant to do anything like that ... well, perhaps $25,000.00 a year. And yes, there were other times, because ... well, what were we going to do, close? Yes, I helped. But never graciously and never wanting to. I stopped many times. I didn't approve of it. I thought it was dreadful. And when it came out soon after the company was founded that I gave money ... well, that just about killed me! I thought I was disgraced, that my career was over. I can only assure you that I never, never bought any of my roles. I got them because I deserved them. If I helped, it was because I thought it would help the company. I wanted to be known only as a dancer. The fact is, I only helped *sometimes.*

"At any rate, when I was asked to be head of Ballet Theatre, I said I'd do it, but not alone. I had met Oliver Smith, who had designed *Fancy Free* for us, and I said I'd go in with him, but only for 1 year, until they could find somebody else. Of course, we've been at it ever since, and in 1975, Antony Tudor joined us as Associate Director—and it's working out just beautifully."*

Lucia Chase's career as a dancer ran from 1938 to 1960. It was a career filled with adventure and happy memories.

"We had *so* much fun in those days!" she said, beaming. "Fokine liked me, and Tudor was very good to me. I was in every Tudor ballet except *Jardin aux lilas* and *Dim Luster.* He made use of my acting ability. Just the other day, Tudor was rehearsing Karena Brock in my part in *Dark Elegies.* At one point, he turned to me and said, 'Aren't you glad you're not doing *that* anymore?' I said 'No! I'm doing every minute of it—inside!' In those years, when we had a role, we kept it. We never got sick. When Tudor did *Pillar of Fire,* I did the Eldest Sister. Nora Kaye and I did *Pillar* for 18 years! Nobody ever did our roles. We gave our last performance in Lisbon in 1960.

"For Fokine I did *Carnaval* and *Petrouchka* and *Les Sylphides*—I and the Prelude on opening nights. *Les Sylphides* was always our opening night ballet. William Dollar danced in it; Karen Conrad did the Mazurka; and Nina Stroganova did the Waltz. But Fokine's *Bluebeard* was really my ballet. It was such an amusing work! There was Bluebeard, danced by Anton Dolin, and Irina Baronova danced the lead. Tudor was The King and I was The Queen—but I had five lovers! And one of them was Jerome Robbins! It was all so much fun!"

What, in effect, was Lucia Chase's role at American Ballet Theatre? It is said that she ruled her company with an iron hand—that, under a veneer of gentility and graciousness, there resided a woman of strong will and no-nonsense toughness.

"Let me say, first of all, that ABT has never been *my* company. I like to say that I'm the head of the complaint department. Of course, my main charge is the dancers. I pick the dancers; I do their contracts—with Oliver Smith, of course. I pick the ballets, the repertory. Then, with Enrique Martinez, the *regisseur,* I set the programs, and I set the casting for the programs. Of course, I have many other people who work with me—Dimitri Romanoff, Daryl Dodson, Scott Douglas, and Michael Lland. But I have to watch all rehearsals, because I am

*Today, Mikhail Baryshnikov is Artistic Director of ABT.

the last word in casting. Dancers come to me with a thousand questions and requests, and we battle over things.

"I have also made it a habit to watch every single performance from the front. You have to see what your dancers are doing; you have to see how they're coming over. Dancers come and tell me how well they're doing, but I prefer to see it for myself.

"I've always had a mind of my own. Of course, I listen to other people. Sometimes, other people can make me change my mind ... a little. At the moment, the company is in wonderful form."

Had Lucia Chase any thoughts on retirement?

"Oh, I couldn't possible leave! If things go wrong, I'd have to be there to try and make them right. No, no, I can't leave."

Clearly, the past 35 years had been vastly fulfilling.

"Oh, yes! I've had 35 years of glorious artistic and personal fulfillment. But what is even more important is that we've become a showcase for American ballet all over the world. That's been the greatest fulfillment of all!"

After Mikhail Baryshnikov became director of ABT in 1980 and until she became ill in 1983, Lucia Chase never missed a Ballet Theatre performance. She died January 9, 1986, at the age of 88.

Lar Lubovich

Photograph by Jack Vartoogian

Lar Lubovitch

Lar Lubovitch is a restless explorer—a dancer and choreographer in search of meaning. To be in his presence is to know a man of a certain diffidence and privacy—someone who cherishes the intellect and eschews the vagaries of undigested thoughts and ideas. Highly intelligent and verbal, Lubovitch offers the image of a man acquainted with the complexities and ambiguities of life. Indeed, this perception of the shadowy meaning of things has been the result of an inherently questioning mind and spirit.

As an artist, Lubovitch has made use of the dramatic events of his personal life, placing some of their effects and repercussions into dances charged with ambivalence and mystery. In works such as *Whirligogs, Time Before the Time After, After the Time Before, Scherzo for Massah Jack, Zig-Zag, Avalanche,* and *Rapid Transit,* among others, a teeming meeting of the psychological and the physical often produces high-voltage aesthetic results. We may not always be given instant accessibility into meaning or intent, but invariably, we are placed in touch with a sensibility that deals with life at its most compelling. Lubovitch equates life with energy, and this energy is at once structured and allowed to create its own metaphysical momentum in his dances.

As a dancer, Lubovitch becomes his own best interpreter.* While his company contains dancers of unusual accomplishment, it is Lubovitch himself who compels special attention: a short, compact man with a face of classic proportion, filled with character and clear-eyed determination. He moves with feline precision, imbuing gesture and the dynamics of motion with a resonance that transcends mere technique. During performance, Lubovitch seems possessed. A compulsive *something* propels him into action, as a terse and astringent lyricism informs his movements, yielding an aura of the obsessively driven. Watching him perform, one intuits that, for Lubovitch, dancing is a metaphor for existence.

As choreographer, Lubovitch is concerned with getting as close as possible to the sinews of his own inner life. He wishes to explore its fabric, unmask its secrets, and lay bare its traps. Critics have not always responded to Lubovitch's work, considering it either too cryptic or too obvious. For the most part, they have missed his point, failing to grasp the stylistic underpinnings of Lubovitch's craft, which present

*Today, Lubovitch has retired from actively performing.

reality only by way of innuendo and suggestion. Indeed, the dynamics of Lubovitch's art are not to be found in any clear-cut representationalism, but in an intriguing combination of abstract and figurative forces.

In person, Lubovitch reflects the tensions found in his work. His mind is quick, alert, nervous; his thoughts race. Born in Chicago in 1943, he claims to have wanted to dance for as long as he can remember. However, it was not until he turned 18 that dancing professionally seemed a viable possibility. Attending Iowa State University, he started out to become a painter. When the José Limón Company visited the university, Lubovitch knew instantly that dancing would be his calling. Soon after, he left Iowa and enrolled for a summer semester in the dance department of Connecticut College. The summer over, he moved to New York and was given a full scholarship in the dance department of the Juilliard School. There, he worked with such artists as Antony Tudor, Louis Horst, Lucas Hoving, Anna Sokolow, Bertram Ross, and Ethel Winter.

"I came to dancing very late," Lubovitch said. "But I had a ferocious determination to achieve certain abilities that the dancers around me already possessed. After Juilliard, I took classes once or twice a week at the Joffrey school and four or five times a week at the Graham school. In time, I began to work with several dance companies—Donald McKayle's, Pearl Lang's, and Glen Tetley's. It was irregular work, because in those days there were no such things as regular seasons or regular tours. Between times, I supported myself as a go-go dancer at Trude Heller's night club in Greenwich Village. I used to stand on a little ledge and hang on to a doorknob to balance myself—and I did that 6 hours a night, 5 nights a week. I needed to work at night, so that I could go to class during the day. I also supported myself as a construction worker. I built bookcases in people's apartments, tore down walls ... things like that."

It was during this period when Lubovitch was 24 that a serious accident put a temporary halt to his career as a dancer. The accident, harrowing in its aftermath, would place Lubovitch's attitude toward himself into perspective, and, ultimately, would clarify the direction of his creative life. Reluctantly recalling the accident, Lubovitch said it was something about which he seldom speaks.

"It happened during the time I was a go-go dancer and a construction worker. One day, I decided to tear down a wall in my own apartment. The crowbar I was using slipped off the wedge I was working on. It was a heavy, two-pronged thing, and it landed on my skull, fracturing it. Of course, at that moment, I didn't realize I had a fractured skull. All I knew was that my forehead was bleeding; so, I put a bandage on it and went back to work. It wasn't until 2 or 3 weeks later that I began to feel ill. I developed bad headaches that grew steadily worse. I went to a hospital, and a doctor there said I had flu symptoms. He gave me flu medicine. The headaches persisted. I went to a private doctor, who recommended I see a psychiatrist. He said my headaches were psychosomatic. The pain became more and more intense. I continued my job at Trude Heller's, and I'd get home so tired that I often found myself lying on the floor behind my closed apartment door or waking up on the bathroom floor after having vomited. I became very, very frightened. I was fearing for my mind. The headaches became so painful that I suffered memory lapses, and my vision became very cloudy. Finally, I could no longer mobilize myself, and a friend brought me to Roosevelt Hospital.

"I was placed in the mental ward. A doctor asked me about the hatred I felt for my mother and father. Well, I didn't hate my mother and father, but he felt that if he could just get me to admit to it, it would clear up my 'problem.' Finally, in the psychiatric ward, it was discovered that something was even *more* wrong with me. A neurosurgeon discovered that something was blocking my vision. It meant exploratory operations. And those led to brain surgery for blood clots. It was fortunate timing, because when they finally did surgery, three-quarters of my brain was covered with blood clots. It was an ordeal—a scary one. Luckily, the rest of me was in very good condition, and I recovered rather quickly. Still, it was a close call. I might not have lived. The effect was, to say the very least, traumatic."

Upon his recovery, Lubovitch plunged into dance with renewed determination. Eager to make up for lost time, he went to his task with a zeal that would prove alienating and somewhat self-destructive.

"I developed an aggression that probably put people off and that probably did not direct me into a path of self-fulfillment. It's so strange, because even while I wasn't thinking positively, some very positive things were taking place. I was growing as a dancer. I was evolving technically, and my energy was enormous. Also, I was rubbing elbows with some very positive people—people who had a lot of integrity. Still, a conflict was set up in me.

"It was produced by my determination to be something I didn't yet understand. I couldn't see that what I wanted to learn was right there before me. My determination was so ferocious that it blinded me. You know, Buddha said, 'The way in is by the door. Why is it that so few of us use it?' Well, the door was right in front of me, but I didn't use it. Later, when I calmed down, I was able to take stock of myself and able to put to use all of the really fine things that had come my way."

The period of Lar Lubovitch's self-recognition occurred in 1965.

He was invited to join the Harkness Ballet, and danced with it for 2 years. In its way, the experience proved both dismaying and rewarding.

"It was while I danced with the Harkness that I realized I wanted to choreograph very seriously. My idea was to choreograph for the Harkness, because they had many fine dancers and many bad works. Well, I was told that I would have to go out and prove myself as a choreographer. I took a leave of absence to do a concert of my own works. When I returned to the Harkness, I was informed that I would not be allowed to choreograph for them. Furthermore, I was informed that if I wanted to go on choreographing, I would have to leave the company—which is what I did. As it turned out, the company folded some months later, and I would have been out anyway. At any rate, I left and tried to raise funds where I could. I choreographed, and I put on concerts. At this point, Paul LePerque and his Foundation helped me. I was very lucky to have his support.

"I continued to work. I gave concerts at the Young Men's Hebrew Association (YMHA) and at the American Theatre Lab. In time, I began receiving invitations to choreograph in Europe. The very first came fro the Bat-Dor Dance Company in Israel. The second came for the Gulbenkian Ballet in Lisbon. The works I created for these two companies went very well, and I began to be recognized in Europe. I suppose I could have gone on to make my choreographic career in Europe, but I soon realized that I wanted to work at home, and I wanted to work with people whose sensibilities were closer to my own."

In 1968, Lubovitch returned to New York and formed a company. Within a year the Lar Lubovitch Dance Company grew into one of the most successful groups in the country.

"Very quickly, and faster than was good for me, the company received both praise and recognition. We had very good tours in Europe and America. But it was all coming at me with enormous velocity. The speed with which things were happening made me realize that I had lost control. By that, I mean I wasn't having the kind of intellectual freedom that was desirable for someone who is trying to choreograph and to create. Also, I had this very powerful aggressive drive, and success seemed very important to me. I kept thinking that this was what I wanted. But all along, I found a continuing inability to exercise my own intellectual freedom over my work. At a certain point, it became clear that the only way to regain my bearings was to stop what I was doing—to pull back for a while and to put myself in order. I folded the company which, of course, upset my dancers and all the people who had put in their time with me. But it was a decision I *had* to make."

Lubovitch withdrew into himself. For an entire year, he neither danced nor choreographed.

"I wanted to learn about myself—not in a mystical sense, but about my body and my brain ... about my physical self. You see, after my brain operation, I developed a strong fear of death. It was this fear of dying that had me going at such a rapid pace. One of the most valuable things I did during this period was to make a study of the brain as an organ. The brain is a fantastic thing! It's something everyone should learn about. This investigation turned out to be a turning point in my life, because I came to realize that the brain is a physiological organ and that thinking is a physiological process. During the year I took off, I learned to think. And I learned that thinking can be understood and can be taught.

"Before that point, I had been guided by a lot of information that had been fed to me by a lot of people—sometimes mistaken information. I was carrying out the mistakes that people had made before me. Well, since that time, I've been thinking for myself, and this has enabled me to gain greater control over my work and my intentions, and I feel more able to stand behind my work. Perhaps the most important thing I've learned is that in order to be truly creative, you must be able to totally override the judgments of others, and, above all, the learned judgments of yourself that you've picked up during your life.

"Well, as that crucial year ended, the pieces started to fall together again. At one point, I was invited to teach at the University of California in Los Angeles (UCLA). I liked the university atmosphere, because all the things I was trying to get together really fermented. Also, there was a certain understanding of work there that was very important and fulfilling to me. It was while I taught at UCLA that I decided to choreograph again and to form a new company."

In 1975, Lubovitch formed his present company. Because of the time he had spent in re-thinking his approach toward himself as a functioning, creative artist, Lubovitch is a man no longer afraid of exposing himself to criticism.

"For me, I choreograph so that I can dance. Right away, the works I choreograph are concerned with dancing to music—to study the music more carefully, to interpret the music in a more enlightened way, to illustrate the music, if you will. Also, I decided no longer to be obscure, no longer to hide my meaning. In the past, I was afraid to show what I really meant—afraid of the judgment of others, afraid I'd be called stupid, or whatever. So, I decided to be direct and not be afraid to say what I wanted to say."

Asked to describe his choreographic methods, Lubovitch's answer was as spontaneous as it was precise:

"I work first from a purely structural standpoint, where I'm really just working on shape. That's where it all begins for me. I begin to build shapes, separate from the music, separate from the ego states that the dancers or I bring in at that moment. I just work on pure visual shape. Then, from that shape, I begin to build motive. After that, I search for the relationship between my shape and the music. I like to think that I build dances *within* the same time of the music, sharing the same time capsule, not necessarily extorting that time identically, but in a correlative way. Then, the combination of the shape, emotional suggestions, and musical correlation is the finished phrase."

Lubovitch maintained that style and originally could neither be willed nor manufactured.

"I am not taken with the idea of originality. The fact is, I'm very happy with the dancing that has come before me and with the many beautiful steps that were handed down to me. I've learned those steps. I've studied classical technique daily. I've studied Graham and Humphrey and Limón [technique]. I try to take in as many ways of dancing as I can absorb. I have a very large vocabulary of contemporary jazz movements. So, I use all of it. I don't see any reason for dividing it up. Jumping and falling and rising, bending and perching— these are all things I know, and they all go together very well. I use it all. I make no pretensions to being an inventor or an innovator. I'm not a trailblazer, because I am the heir to a great fortune of movement, and I'm very happy to have inherited this fortune.

"As for originality, I can only say this much: Whenever people go into themselves to seek the core of themselves, they will find an original note, because every human being is original. Each person has something that will not be matched by anyone else. I dig into the core of myself all of the time and look for the kernel—the seed. If I do that, then I am an original, just as all people are. For this reason, as much as any other, I do not feel motivated to be an original in my work. I search for the originality in myself as a human being. And if I find that originality, then my work will be original, because it is a direct expression of myself."

Ghislaine Thesmar

Ghislaine Thesmar with Adam Luders
Photograph by Costas

Ghislaine Thesmar

Imagine a frail, slender girl, the only child of a French diplomat, spending her formative years in Peking, Cuba, Indonesia, India, Morocco—a wide-eyed little French girl, born in Peking in 1943, wandering the globe, her sensibilities shaped by myriad exotic images, landscapes, languages, climates, and traditions. No one, least of all she herself, could have foreseen that this delicate, highly impressionable, continually uprooted youngster would one day emerge as Ghislaine Thesmar, an *étoile* of the Paris Opéra Ballet, and a special favorite of George Balanchine.

And yet, despite her peripatetic young life, Thesmar was exposed to an atmosphere that nurtured her responses to art, to music, and to all that would in later years coalesce and bring into full flower an artist of unusual sensitivity and refinement. She may have been uprooted, but she was loved. No mater where her family relocated, home always meant hearing her father playing Chopin, Ravel, or Mozart on the piano (he had studied with Cortot and Marguerite Long) or watching her mother paint delicate Oriental landscapes inspired by Chinese masters. And, after all, being a diplomat's daughter *could* be full of surprises.

When her father's diplomatic duties took the family to Havana, Thesmar had her first glimpse of ballet. She recalls it as something utterly strange, mysterious, and beautiful: "I must have been 5 or 6 years old. My mother took me to see the Alicia Alonso Ballet, and I have a flash of recollection of Alonso in the Mazurka in *Les Sylphides*—the jumps! I just couldn't believe such a thing could be done! But there was this creature rising in space ... it was an incredible vision!"

Speaking fluent English and looking trim and elegant in a silk print, the ballerina offered the image of cosmopolitan sophistication. Intelligent, witty, and with just a touch of world-weariness, Thesmar looked back on her life with amused incredulity.

"Really, considering the complexity of my childhood, it's a wonder I achieved anything at all! I mean, soon after that first magical glimpse of Alonso, we went to live in Indonesia—a desert as far as ballet was concerned. Although my mother had made me take some lessons with Alonso's sister in Cuba, I forgot everything I learned, and nothing at all happened until several years when my father was transferred to India. There, I attended an English school and among the teachers was a lovely lady who gave twice-weekly classes in tap dancing and Scottish jigs! Well, that was my next exposure to dance. It was quite a lot of fun but, of course, it wasn't ballet. Anyway, while we were living in India my parents decided that I really needed to know something of my French heritage. The fact was, I barely spoke the language and, as I had a grandmother living in Paris, they sent me to stay with her so that I might absorb some French culture and become fluent in French—and off I went. By this time I was already 14, and when I landed in Paris I felt absolutely miserable. I was alone; I knew no one; and I found Paris very cold and austere. To give me *some* pleasure, my grandmother allowed me to take some ballet classes—and that was a solace."

Young Thesmar's stay in Paris was short-lived, however. Within a year, her father received a new assignment. He would be posted in Morocco and, having located an excellent French school, he sent for his daughter, who would continue her studies there.

"Again, I found myself in a strange land. But this time I had much better luck with finding a ballet teacher. She was an ex-ballerina who had danced with the Paris Opéra Ballet. What was marvelous was the fact that she thought I had talent. She insisted that I work with her three times a week and took a real interest in me. Of course, I still considered dancing as something of a pleasurable pastime—if I had talent it might, perhaps, lead me *somewhere* ... but it was all very vague. I mean, I was 15, and the thought of dancing professionally never really occurred to me. Still, this teacher spoke to my parents and told them that if we ever got back to Paris I should enter into the competition for admission into the Paris Conservatoire. She made them aware of my potential and said that I had the makings of a fine dancer. Well, that sounded very exciting, but I had little confidence in my own abilities and didn't take it all that seriously.

"Then, a marvelous thing happened. This teacher made it possible for me to see a film of Galina Ulanova, the great star of the Bolshoi Ballet, dancing in *Giselle.* I was simply overwhelmed. I suddenly saw what dancing could be. It was watching Ulanova that completely changed my life. From that moment on, I realized that dancing could hold real meaning in one's life. I could see the dimension that a life in dance could offer. Suddenly, I knew what I wanted."

When in 1958 the Thesmar family finally found itself back in Paris, Ghislaine duly entered the competition for entrance into the Conservatoire. Two hundred girls competed, and only five were chosen. Ghislaine Thesmar was the very first.

"Frankly, I was shocked. I mean, I had a good line, natural arms, but no technique at all. Anyway, I entered the Conservatoire, and in addition to full ballet training, we received a complete academic education, all of it paid for by the government. I remained at the Conservatoire for 3 years and emerged with a State Diploma and an intense love for dance. I was not yet 18, and the normal thing would have been to audition for a place with the Paris Opéra Ballet. But I felt this would be a mistake, because I knew I was still too weak. Because I had entered the Conservatoire quite late, I felt I had a lot of catching up to do. I wanted more experience. What I did was to audition for the Grand Ballet de Marquis de Cuevas, and I was accepted as a member of the corps. Now this was 1961, and it was the year Rudolf Nureyev had defected and was now dancing with de Cuevas in Paris. Well, you can imagine how exciting that was, being part of performances with Rudy. Watching him was incredible. He danced with such passion, such fire! He gave 200 percent of himself ... and we were all infected by his incredible presence and magnetism."

Thesmar proved a welcome addition to the company. She danced in a repertory that included Nijinska's version of *The Sleeping Beauty* ("We lived off that ballet!") and in works by Serge Lifar, William Dollar, George Balanchine, and others. A tall, lithe, exceptionally musical dancer, she brought a special lyricism to even the smallest parts, and in time she found herself advancing within the ranks. Hungry for improvement, she worked privately with Serge Peretti, an outstanding Paris-based teacher, and carefully observed the mastery of such ballerinas as Yvette Chauviré and Marilyn Jones, who had joined the de Cuevas Ballet as guest artists. The company toured extensively, but after the Marquis died in 1961, it became evident that the company's own life would be short-lived. While on tour in Greece in 1962, management informed its dancers that the de Cuevas Ballet would be dissolved, and Thesmar returned to Paris.

"We were all dispersed. I went back to Paris and continued working with Peretti, because I still needed to improve, get stronger, and really be on top of my technique. At one point, I received an invitation from George Skibine, who, with his wife, Marjorie Tallchief, had formed a small group which would be dancing at the Festival in Aix-en-Provence. There were eight dancers; one of them was Pierre Lacotte, whom I would marry some years later. Well, we danced at the Festival—Skibine staged his version of *Les Noces*—and then we toured. This went on for a while, and it was good to be with a small group, because the chance of dancing *all* of the time was there, and it gave me a measure of confidence.

"Pierre Lacotte was an interesting man ... very commanding and full of ambition. Eventually, he decided to form his own group, and he asked me to join it. The group became known as the Ballet National Jeunesses Musicales de France, and it consisted of 12 dancers. We toured endlessly and became quite successful."

As it turned out, in Thesmar, Pierre Lacotte had found his Galatea.

He saw her beauty, her insouciance, her talent, and that special something that merely needed the touch and guiding hand of someone who truly believed in her. Lacotte would become her Pygmalion; he would bring her to life. And his love for her would give depth and dimension to a dancer still untouched by personal passion or experience.

"I was 20 and Pierre was 31. He set out to form me. You see, I knew I loved dancing, but I had no real ambition. I did not see myself as a super-ballerina—a star. I worked, but I never fought to get ahead. My temperament was passive but Pierre was just the opposite. Well, Pierre felt that I should prove myself to the utmost and, I must say, it was wonderful meeting someone who wanted things for me more than I did. So, he made me work with his group for 5 long years. We toured 7 months out of the year and danced four ballets every single night, mostly one-night stands. It was unbelievably tiring, but it was also the sort of apprenticeship that really made you discover your artistic boundaries. You learned your limitations as well as how far you could reach. So, I tried everything. All styles came my way—from the most classical to the most avant-garde—and I danced and danced and danced! Lacotte gave me tremendous confidence, simply because he believed in me. He instilled in me *his* conception of what dance should be, and I followed it unquestioningly.

"It was only later, with Balanchine, that I liberated myself. But Pierre Lacotte formed me, gave me my identity, and made me realize the extent of my capabilities. The fact is, Lacotte was part of a heritage I really knew nothing about. I mean, he trained at the Paris Opéra since the age of 9. He was part of a tradition that saw Balanchine coming to the Paris Opéra in 1947 with Tamara Toumanova and Maria Tallchief ... he was there during the best period and knew so much more than I did. Through Lacotte I discovered the world of ballet and theater, and I was enthralled. At any rate, in 1968 we married ... and we are married still."

The 5 years with Lacotte's Jeunesses Musicales proved invaluable for Ghislaine Thesmar. Her body became an instrument able to encompass the widest variety of styles. Under Lacotte's watchful and caring supervision, she became strong, fleet, and her movements now contained a clarity that gave shape and substance to every choreographic persuasion. Her lean grace and musicality had been welded to great technical security, and she emerged from Lacotte's tutelage a full-fledged and entirely dazzling ballerina.

"I cannot deny that working with Pierre was the turning point of my artistic life. But there finally came a moment when I simply needed something different. I certainly needed to get away from Pierre's group. The constant touring had become intolerable ... I just had to move elsewhere, and I needed to be on my own. I found my chance in Canada.

"I accepted an invitation from Les Grands Ballets Canadiens. It was a good move—up to a point. Unfortunately, I had a very bad rapport with the company's director, Ludmilla Chiriaeff. She was one of those women who functioned very well in terms of getting money and support for the company, but I'm afraid she was a very bad director. She had poor judgment, and I felt she was incompetent. Luckily, her balletmaster was Fernand Nault, with whom I got along very well. Nault was a professional, to everyone's great relief he quickly succeeded Madame Chiriaeff as director—and that was wonderful.

"It was also wonderful just staying put in one place. I had the good fortune of working with John Butler and other fine choreographers. I had the opportunity of dancing Balanchine's *Theme and Variations,* as well as the classics. Well, I stayed with Les Grande Ballets for 1 year—until 1969, at which point I returned to Paris and began to work with Roland Petit. Roland did not really have a company, but would gather one together and go on tour. He created a beautiful ballet for me and Cyril Atanassoff called *Rendezvous,* and I was just about to dance the lead in another new work based on Alban Berg's *Lulu* when Roland fell ill. The project never materialized, and the group disbanded.

"Suddenly, I was stranded, and I had a hard time of it. My husband felt I shouldn't do just anything in France, that if I were going to perform, it would have to be with a company of real distinction. Well ... what I did was to give myself 2 years of further training. I worked privately with Yvette Chauviré, and just gave myself over to intense study.

"Then, the most extraordinary thing happened. My husband undertook to write a book on Marie Taglioni (1804–1884), and during the course of his research, he came across some very rare manuscripts that gave the most detailed account of the original version of *La Sylphide,* which had been choreographed by Marie's father, Fillippo Taglioni (1777–1871), in 1832. All the original steps were recorded exactly the way Marie had danced them when the ballet had its premiere at the Paris Opéra. There were also completely accurate descriptions of the scenery, done by Ciceri, and of the costumes, created by Lami. Pierre also obtained the score for the original *Sylphide,* which had been composed by Schneitzhoeffer. Well, these papers were an incredible *trouvail;* they had all been dispersed and now belonged to the relatives of the Taglionis, whom my husband looked up.

"Pierre resolved to reconstruct the ballet in its original form and proposed it to French television which accepted the idea. I was chosen to dance the Sylph and Michael Denard danced James. Well, the TV film turned out to be an incredible success, and it proved to be a major turning point in my career."

Following the television premiere of Lacotte's reconstruction of *La Sylphide,* the film was shown to the management of the Paris Opéra Ballet who considered it something of a masterpiece. They instantly invited Lacotte to stage the work for the company and, in an unprecedented gesture, invited Ghislaine Thesmar to repeat her role as the Sylph.

"It was an unbelievable invitation, because no French dancer had ever been invited to come to the Paris Opéra Ballet as a guest artist. I mean, you're either a French dancer already *in* the company or you're a foreign guest artist, in which case you may fulfill a guest engagement. Well, I was the exception. I received a guest-artist contract to do three performances of *La Sylphide*—and I was scared to death. As it turned out, I had an incredible success. The press was glowing, and I really created a bit of a stir. As a result of all this, the Paris Opéra Ballet asked me to join them as a permanent member—*and* as a principal.

"Of course, this was also most unusual, because at the Paris Opéra you must rise through the ranks, and it takes years! But, in 1972, I entered the company as principal dancer, and it was fantastic. Of course, there were problems. My first 2 years at the Opéra were extremely difficult. I was made to feel that I was stepping on other people's toes; it was quite unbearable. But I tried to assimilate myself as best I could, learning all their repertory, dancing in all the classics, and trying to do my best. Throughout, my principal partner was Michael Denard, and the public seemed to respond to us.

"Then, another miraculous thing happened. George Balanchine came to the Paris Opéra to stage several of his works, including his *Chaconne.* He had chosen three couples to learn the lead roles, and Michael and I were among them. Well, he chose us for the premiere, and that's how I came under Balanchine's wing. When he returned to stage a Stravinsky program, he gave me *Agon,* and when he came to do a Ravel program, I danced in his *La Valse* and *Tzigane.*"

It was easy to see why Balanchine found Ghislaine Thesmar suitable to dance in his works. She was intensely musical and her body followed in the precepts of the so-called Balanchine dancer—the long legs, the long flowing arms, the quicksilver speed, and the sort of flexibility that could easily execute the abstract geometry of Balanchine's choreographic genius. Balanchine also responded to Thesmar's keen intelligence and even more to her great willingness to place her body in the service of his works. Indeed, so impressed was the choreographer with the ballerina's performances that he promptly invited her to join the New York City Ballet as guest artist.

"From the first Balanchine said, 'Come and dance with us.' Well, I thought he was just being charming, but in 1975 he actually called me from New York and said, 'Are you free from this to this period?' And, of course, I made myself free and flew to New York during the summer 1975 season and danced *Concerto Barocco* with Peter Martins, as well as *Sonatine*. All in all, I learned 12 Balanchine ballets, and that's how my City Ballet association began.

"The fact is, Balanchine *really* liberated me. He liberated me on my own home ground—the Paris Opéra Ballet—and as a dancer in general. He gave me a security I never really experienced before, and it now colors everything I do as an artist. For example, he told me that in order to dance well, you must be in harmony with yourself. He said, 'You have to *feel* good in order to *look* good.' Of course, I understood that quite early, but, through Balanchine, the notion triggered other concepts, such as the idea of *losing* oneself in a role rather than *finding* oneself. You see, for me, dancing in any work means a kind of dying and living. I never try to find myself in any role. To find Ghislaine Thesmar in a role has never interested me. I live *through* the feelings of a choreographer and through the feeling of the music. Balanchine has been of enormous help in giving me the courage to lose myself and to transform myself into a *being* that dances. It is perhaps my most valuable achievement."

Thesmar has also had occasion to work with Jerome Robbins, both at the Paris Opéra and at the New York City Ballet, notably in *Afternoon of a Faun* and *In G Major*.

"Jerry is a very different personality. It's another universe, another sensibility, and I love working with him. I find him excessively human and excessively vulnerable. Because he battles with himself so much, he probably finds it necessary to do battle with his interpreters as well. But the results! They are a dream! There is great naturalness in his dances—an ease that is quite deceptive, because to dance Robbins correctly is extremely difficult. It is a challenge, but the rewards are very great."

In 1985, Thesmar was awarded the prestigious chevalier de la Légion d'Honneur, and, along with Pierre Lacotte, was appointed Director des Ballets de Monte Carlo. In 1988, she returned to the Paris Opéra Ballet as both dancer and teacher.

"Really, my career has been miraculous," said Thesmar in conclusion. "I've been extremely lucky and at times this luck scares me half to death. Finally, it's all about being receptive to life ... that counts for much! Of course, life has its dark side. Nothing is perfect in this world.

But I don't ask myself too many questions on that score. I'm not one of those people who broods and worries. If I have wounds I leave them be, because, like most wounds, they usually heal by themselves. That's been my experience so far. In the meantime, I dance, because dancing has always been my salvation ... the ultimate freedom!"

Daniel Nagrin

Photograph by Beverly Owen; Courtesy of Daniel Nagrin

Daniel Nagrin

On a cold January afternoon, I made my way to a loft located at 550 Broadway in lower Manhattan. I entered the old building to keep an appointment with a dancer who had invited me to watch him execute two dances of his own invention.

The dancer was not a young man. The weight of life was clearly discernible in a man who, even as he greeted me with utmost cordiality, seemed oddly distant, strangely bound by an aura of isolation, somehow immersed in a vast solitude. This sense of diffidence and emotional distance was abetted by an appearance at once forbidding and curiously hypnotizing. A face of stern and even bitter expression, with features suggesting a stylized Oriental mask, revealed both intellectual depth and an immense introspection. This was not a person who looked at the world lightly. This was a man of thought—a man of unusual complexity and strong feeling. This was Daniel Nagrin, the great loner of American dance.

Nagrin, born in 1917, is approaching an age when most male dancers have long retired. Yet, he presents the physical image of someone years younger. His body is strong, trim, lithe, quick, and supple. Only at closest proximity does one note the years, and even then, the semblance of age is communicated more on a psychological than on a physical level. It is as if from earliest youth, Nagrin had been invested by the resonance of age. When age did come, it remained a natural extension of the past and thus rendered the passage of time mysteriously unnoticeable. This startling manifestation was, of course, most evident when Nagrin danced.

A single chair had been placed at one end of Nagrin's large studio-loft. He motioned me to sit and, after adjusting and starting the tape recorder, began the first of the two promised dances. In an instant, the space before me became charged by a presence that announced a heightened meeting of movement and sound. Nagrin, in practice clothes, offered his famous *Spanish Dance*—his impression of a Flamenco dance. He had composed it in 1948 to the music of Genevieve Pitot. What met the eye was a flamenco no real flamenco dancer had ever devised. Nagrin transmuted the dance into a metaphor, a parable of existence, in which the jutting, staccato thrusts of the movements became drenched in myriad alternating emotions. Without ever abandoning the dignity of the Spanish style, Nagrin produced what amounted to a synthesis of its varying emotional underpinnings. With extraordinary economy, his body conveyed all that lay beneath the dance: from tenderness to pride to sadness to excitement to brutality. The dance seemed to follow in the natural dynamics of a turning prism, its colors moving slowly or swiftly within its forceful vortex.

The flamenco done, Nagrin quickly turned to the next dance, a work called *Strange Hero.* It lasted but 4 minutes, but within that brief timespan, a new set of powerful emotions were laid bare. This was a solo akin to a play—perhaps by Pinter—in which the inner self was explored by way of dance. It told a story that could be read on many levels. Was this man a killer? A fugitive? A madman pursued by his inner demons? Looking into an imaginary mirror, Nagrin exposed the nerve ends (or paranoia) of a character in the throes of despair. Evoking invisible characters, he lurched from corner to center to corner, now crouching in fear, now bursting out with reckless daring, in a last effort to save his life or sanity. This was yet another transformation in which dance translated into pure theater.

The dancer next set up a screen to show me a film on which a number of other solos had been recorded, most of them jazz solos, a form Nagrin has perfected throughout the years. Dances such as *Jazz Three Times, Blue Man, Bounce Boy, Bob Man,* and *Man of Action* made clear Nagrin's mastery of an idiom that he has made his own. How oddly seductive to watch this somewhat dour man inhabiting the carefree, biting, languorous, or smooth-and-easy idioms of jazz dancing! But with singular artistry and authenticity, the genre came stunningly to life, as head, eyes, shoulders, torso, arms, and legs produced a counterpoint of subtle rhythms, in which an infallible sense of timing and an infectious wit informed every gesture and movement.

Daniel Nagrin has been a performing artist since 1940, and, since 1957, has made a major career as one of the country's leading solo dancers. Years of touring, lecturing, and teaching have brought him into contact with a vast public that has invariably responded to Nagrin's capacity for single-handedly filling a stage with disparate and fascinating characters. Critical accolades and standing ovations have attended Nagrin's tours.

What amazes is that Nagrin not only dances alone, but is his own manager, set, and lighting designer, as well as sound engineer. As he put it, "I go out *really* alone: no stage manager, no business manager, et cetera, and it's quite a thing to get off a plane in Fort Hays, Kansas, with my tape recorder over my shoulder, looking for someone I don't know who is looking for me. And then: Zap! I am in a world that becomes my only world for a day, a half-week, or a week, designing, setting, and directing the hanging of lights; teaching cues and directing the layout of the sound system with which I travel; performing the concerts; giving lecture-demonstrations, workshops, and master classes."

Nagrin's distinguished life as a dancer has long been a matter of record. His own recollections of that life, however, have not been made public. It was therefore a rare privilege to speak to Nagrin about his career. Hesitant, at first, to speak openly about his life and work, he became progressively more open and candid.

"I never had any desire to become a dancer," Nagrin began. "I just wanted to learn the box step, which was the key to social dancing in my day. So, I learned the box step. Then, while I was still in high school, I had gotten into a period where I wasn't out in the streets with my friends. My family and I moved around a great deal in New York (where I was born), and it just became one gang too many to get into. So, I spent a great deal of time in the house, and I'd study a bit, and then I'd get up and throw myself about—flip on the radio and do some crazy movements. One Sunday, I put on the radio, and there was some Armenian music playing, and it caught me. I moved with it, and I was just flying about, on air, and it became a very exciting experience."

Instinct goaded the youngster into seeking out and exploring further the mysteries of those first dance sensations. At a party, he observed two women engaged in an argument. One of these, Nagrin recalled, was in a deep contraction, hovering over the floor. She was demonstrating something to a friend who obviously had no use for what she was seeing. Nagrin approached the woman in her unusual exertion, and asked her what she was doing. "Dancing!" she replied. Instantly, Nagrin asked where he could learn such dancing. It would take him an entire year to find out.

He joined The New Dance Group, where he began to study modern dance. What he learned seemed less than enthralling. "I remember talking to a young fellow there, and saying to him, 'There must be more to modern dance than this!' He said, 'There is.' So, we pulled up chairs, and he proceeded to give a lecture on modern dance right then and there, explaining the Hanya Holm technique, which came out of Mary Wigman's teachings, with its spatial consciousness, and the Humphrey-Weidman technique, with its fall and recovery, and the Graham technique, with its contraction and release. He demonstrated as he went along. When he got to Graham's contraction and release, I said, "Where is *that* taught?," because I had already been doing that on my own. I switched classes at The New Dance Group and found myself the only male in a class of girls studying the Graham technique. When the term was over, I began to work with a woman by the name of Ray Moses. It was on Ray that Martha Graham had worked out her *Lamentation,* seeing what it looked like from the outside. Ray was in

Martha's first expanded company, and from her I got a profound connection with dance. But even then, I never had any intention of becoming a dancer. In fact, I was on my way to becoming a psychiatrist, taking courses at City College. I was still young, just at the point of turning 19."

Nagrin worked with Ray Moses for nearly a year. "She was a wonderful woman and, even today, when I teach, I find sentences springing from my mouth that I know came from her—things like, 'Your arms should move with the architecture and weight of your legs.' Or, 'Your legs should have the specificity and delicacy and tactile sensitivity of your arms and hands.' She was full of things like that. And she could teach a class of 25 people, and each of us was convinced that she was there for us personally. Then, she more or less retired, and, of course, I thought it an utter betrayal of me that she should live her own life."

All along, Nagrin attended City College. He graduated, and, with an additional year of postgraduate study, he emerged, not with a degree in psychiatry, but in health education. Concurrently, he studied ballet with Elizabeth Anderson-Ivantzova and took modern classes with Helen Tamiris, Martha Graham, Hanya Holm, Anna Sokolow, Nenette Charisse, and Edward Caton. These courses of study left their indelible personal and professional marks on Daniel Nagrin who, by the age of 23, had finally come to realize that dance would be his life.

The dancer recalled his encounter with those who shaped his creative thinking, his career, and who ultimately propelled him toward the solo dance form. To begin with, there were Martha Graham and Anna Sokolow; Nagrin made his professional debut in 1940 with the Sokolow company.

"In some subtle way, Anna and I were on similar tracks," Nagrin said. "We both had an interest in the world and in people—an awareness that the world not only could be a better place, but that people should be aware when it is *not* so good. We both believed that in one's art you could perhaps not necessarily change things, but at least point a wavering finger in a certain direction. So, that's something I garnered from Anna Sokolow. What one gets from a person like Martha Graham is not easily summarized in words. One could say that what she gives you is the unequivocal investment of your whole being. Still, what I didn't connect with and what led to my ultimately working in the solo form was the inherent competitiveness in those situations. It was always in the air, and it is an aspect of our field that I have always been repelled by. The fact is, I never had any desire to be better than anybody else—no sense that I was going to top this one or that one. In Martha's classes, I could feel that people weren't always doing something necessarily for themselves, but very often for Martha's grace. Well, I played with that for a bit, but I didn't care for it."

A turning point in Nagrin's attitude toward himself came during one such class, when a young dancer turned to him and said, 'Danny, what are you *really* going to do?' Nagrin answered, 'Why, I'm going to dance!' When the girl said, 'Really? Why?,' Nagrin stopped short, and considered the question.

"Suddenly, my mind flew over the field of dance, and I saw all the men who were working then. In a sweep, I could see Charles Weidman, José Limón, Merce Cunningham, and Erick Hawkins, and I said to this girl, 'Because I'm going to be dealing with things that the others aren't going to touch!' This was a moment of revelation, and it gave me incredible strength."

What these other dancers were not going to touch was jazz dancing. In 1941, Daniel Nagrin joined Unity House, a performance organization that brought together dancers, choreographers, stage directors, playwrights, actors, and others. Nagrin auditioned as a dancer, but was deemed less than electrifying by Unity House's resident choreographer, Helen Tamiris. Disappointed but not discouraged, Nagrin went away and set about to improve his jazz technique.

"I worked with a woman named Sue Remos and also with Fanya Chochem. From Sue, I learned the foundations of jazz. We used to go to the Savoy Ballroom and dance together and watch for hours. Those dancers were so brilliant and so elegant! I worked with Sue and Fanya for 1 year. At the conclusion of the year, I auditioned again at Unity House, mainly because Sue Remos was going there, and I wanted her to become my partner. There was a lot of resistance about my getting into Unity House, but, because someone dropped out, I was accepted. I danced a duet with Sue Remos, and this time, Helen Tamiris, toward whom I felt rather hostile, liked what she saw."

As it turned out, Nagrin's association with the volatile Helen Tamiris would prove seminal in Nagrin's development as an artist. The relationship would culminate in marriage, and, ultimately, in the formation of the Tamiris-Nagrin Dance Company.

"Working with Tamiris was quite disturbing," said Nagrin. "She taught classes, but it wasn't Graham—it was Tamiris. And she worked very much from impulse. *That's* what was disturbing, because I had been brought up on a solid dance technique and background, and I couldn't find any sense of organization in the way she was teaching. Still, she had a way of making sense out of it. I remember working on a dance called *Shake It and Break It,* to a recording of Sidney Bechet, and I was having a lot of trouble with it. Tamiris said, 'For whom are you doing this dance?' In my naive way, I answered, 'Well, I want to use it in a concert, and I also want to use it for shows and as an audition piece.' She said, 'You can't get everything out of *one* piece.' And in the course of our discussion, she began to walk around the room, talking about acting and dancing and how they could be one. This 15-minute talk was the turning point of my work.

"Tamiris would throw questions at me. She'd talk about the Stanislavsky method of acting and link it with dance, and I came to understand how Stanislavsky would ask very simple questions that required very complex answers and an enormous amount of work. So Tamiris would work with me within that context, and, suddenly, instead of trying to do something that would look attractive or that she would approve of, I caught on to the person functioning in the world of movement-metaphors, instead of words. Even though my technique was then still quite limited, I began to do things that were virtuosic, and I could do them with conviction. Anyway, from that point on, Tamiris and I became linked professionally and personally for many years."

Helen Tamiris's studio on Lafayette Street became the scene of numerous concerts. She and Nagrin offered performances that, early on, caught the eye of the manager of the Rainbow Room. The two dancers were engaged to perform a nightclub act.

"I didn't like that one bit," recalled Nagrin. "Even though I knew that people like Charles Weidman and Jack Cole had danced at the Waldorf, it just wasn't for me. Anyway, I was saved from it all when I was drafted into the service in 1942."

Nagrin received a medical discharge, due to poor eyesight, and upon returning to civilian life, rejoined Helen Tamiris, who had become interested in choreographing for the Broadway stage.

"Tamiris was a very careful craftsperson. She learned that she could work very quickly, and bring life and dignity to the Broadway musical. We did two shows that never reached New York. One was called *Mariette,* about the French underground, and the other was *Stove-Pipe Hat,* which was about Abraham Lincoln. Then, finally, *Up in Central Park* made it, and then Tamiris did *Showboat,* which was a smash. Oscar Hammerstein saw me dance, and he gave me the lead dance role in *Annie Get Your Gun.* I was the chief Indian, and the Indian dance that Tamiris did for me had a lot of excitement, a lot of dignity. Then came the costume, and it consisted of a slightly indecent little flap—and that was it! I was embarrassed by it, because it wasn't in the spirit of the piece. I felt like a trained monkey.

"Still, it was my first success on Broadway—it was 1946—and no sooner did I get it, than I wanted to stop dancing. Even while performing, I began to study acting, playwrighting, anything, so that I wouldn't have to dance. Well, what I realized was that what I didn't want to do was dance on Broadway. There were things between the intention of the choreographer and what finally came out that proved demoralizing. I mean, you were dealing with people—producers—of questionable taste or of such remorseless need for super-success that it stopped being about art. It was depressing. Nevertheless I kept going from show to show for a long time. I went into *Lend an Ear*; Tamiris did *Touch and Go,* and I danced in that with Pearl Lang. Then came *Plain and Fancy,* and I got the Donaldson Award for Best Male Dancer of the 1954–55 season. The following year, I choreographed *Volpone,* which was directed by Gene Frankel, and that was also a success."

Daniel Nagrin's career as a dancer in Broadway musicals would probably have continued far longer, had he not attended a solo dance performance given by Paul Draper.

"I was bombed by the beauty of his work," Nagrin said. "The curtains closed, the houselights went up, and I went right through the curtain to see him. I said to him, 'Paul, you gave the most magnifi ... ' and he interrupted me and said, 'Why aren't you doing solo concerts?' He told me there was work out there for a serious dancer. Well, between 1944 and 1955, I was making and performing solo dances all the time—at Connecticut College and elsewhere—but I would do two or three pieces, and there would be something else on the program. I never thought I could sustain a *whole* solo concert, because of the tremendous energy it requires.

"Well, Paul said to me, 'Look, you go out with a pianist, do two dances, and then let the pianist go on, and after that come back for two more dances, and then it's time for intermission. Then you open the second act with a dance and a poem. You dance and talk, and it's much easier. Your pianist does another turn, you do two more dances, and the concert is over.' And that's just what I did. I built my first concerts on that format. I'll never forget the first concert I did. The pianist was Sylvia Marshall. Tamiris went up with me to a college near Boston, called Wheaton. It flashed through my mind that I wouldn't be able to sustain it—that I was going to come back in a wheelchair. What happened was that when we were coming back, little snakes of spasm began to curl through my back, and my whole back was just wild. But as I began to do more and more concerts, this phenomenon went away. These days, I don't go off the stage at all."

Daniel Nagrin gave his first solo concert in 1957 at the age of 40. Throughout the years, he created a large body of work, including such dances as *Strange Hero, Man of Action, Nineteen Upbeats, Indeterminate Figure, Path, A Gratitude,* and perhaps his most famous work, the full-length *Peloponnesian War.* In these dances, Nagrin created a microcosm of social, political, and psychological attitudes that through dance mirrored the human condition. How does Nagrin go about creating these brilliant, self-sustaining works?

"Well, I read books. I look at people. I listen to music. In my dances, I'm often dealing with certain moments in life, where an individual has to cope with something as an individual—to face up to something or to do something that entails personal responsibility. In a certain context, you could say that the spine of my work is what is happening between people. That's what I deal with. Sometimes, it may have a political context. I know that in our field this area is regarded as somewhat questionable. In the early days, all the modern dancers were terribly aware of historical context and historical movement. Well, I believe that any aesthetic gesture is also a social or political gesture. Much of the modern dance movement wants to disclaim this and say that it is interested only in pure movement, or pure beauty, or whatever. But I say, what is more political than the love between a man and a woman?

"Certainly, women have finally picked up their heads and said, 'Now wait a minute! This is not the way I want the terms of love to be.' So, you see, the relationship between a man and a woman in a classic pas de deux is a political relationship. I mean, it's heavy politics when a woman has to be picked up—lifted—by a man. As I say to young women, 'When you go on a trip with a man, and he puts your bags in the car, he is getting exercise, and you are not. He is getting stronger, and you are not.' We all know that throughout our civilization, the fact that one person is stronger than another means that certain rules that are not visible are still active. So, I do not know what isn't political and what isn't social.

"But as to my dances. When I compose them, I don't use the mirror a great deal. If I sometimes am unsure of what I'm doing or if I feel my intention is being expressed in a blurry way, then I look at the mirror. At other times, I ask people to look at what I'm doing. When Tamiris and I were together, I would often show things to her, and these were very strange experiences. Though I trusted her eye and her taste explicitly, she had a very rough way of expressing herself. I would start to argue with her, and then she would say, 'Well, I'm not going to criticize you or even look at you.' It was a routine that we had. She'd always exaggerate some point. Later, I would find out that she didn't mean it quite the way she had put it, but by then, the scar tissue would already have formed. In recent years, I've had friends and lovers I'd show things to. I would hear what they had to say and then decide ... maybe yes, maybe no ... and just go on. When you work alone, you develop a certain sense of taste. You say to yourself, 'I don't like that,' and you'd throw it out. I've thrown out many dances."

In 1960, Daniel Nagrin and Helen Tamiris formed the Tamiris-Nagrin Dance Company. It would last 3 years. Nagrin chose not to dwell on the experience. "It turned out to be not an ideal way of working for me. I really don't like choreographing for other people, and I don't like other people choreographing for me. The way I would work with Tamiris is that she would throw out a situation, and I would improvise around it. I didn't feel for a minute that I did the choreography. I knew it was her choreography. Anyway, our company met with a lot of financial problems—it was difficult. And, as I said, I didn't really like telling people what to do, and I didn't like being told what to do."

Helen Tamiris died of cancer in 1966. By then, she and Nagrin were no longer together. "Tamiris and I worked together from 1941 to 1963, and I'm not sure that I want to discuss the personal aspects of our relationship. We separated in 1963. We were never divorced. Just separated."

Nagrin continued to concertize and to compose solo dances throughout the '60s, and, in 1970, began work with The Workgroup, an improvisational dance company, which he developed and which led him to explore new areas of body communication. "I felt that through improvisation, I had found a level of work that made me feel very good. It made me understand why I had had such difficulty choreographing. Through improvisation, I challenged people to follow through on certain tasks that I would set up. It was a very good experience, and it lasted for 3 years."

Daniel Nagrin has been involved in numerous other activities and projects. Along with wide concert tours throughout the States, Europe, and the Pacific, he has taught body movement to actors at the National Theatre Institute in Waterford, CT, chaired the dance committee that devised a Bachelor of Fine Arts in dance for the Leonard Davis Center for the Arts at the City College of New York, conducted dozens of workshops and residences around the country, and in 1985 completed the 15-hour *Nagrin Videotape Library of Dance,* which was presented at New York City's Joyce Theatre by the Dance Collection of the New York Public Library. Currently, Nagrin is on the faculty of Arizona State University's Dance Department. His book, *How to Dance Forever,* was published in 1988.

Asked to comment on his contribution to dance, Nagrin approached the question with characteristic ambiguity.

"I have a resistance to articulate it, because on one level I don't know, and on another, I do. When I teach, for instance, I tell young dancers that I think it's an error to know what your style is. Once you know what your style is, you are likely to get locked into it. As for me, once I try to define myself, I feel I'll be locked into that definition. When I watch myself on film, I have a fierce need to forget what I've seen, because what I've seen was a certain person with a certain style, and I don't want to have to deal with my memory of that.

"On one level, I know precisely where I'm at, and I know precisely where I have shaken some people so that they could say, 'Oh, that's possible!' or 'Oh, that's an area that's exciting to look at!' On the other hand, there is much that I do that I don't know anything about. So you see, definitions are dangerous. The point is, rather than defining myself, I'd rather keep on working. Finally, work and more work is what it's all about!"

Cynthia Gregory

Photograph by Gregory Heisler; Courtesy of American Ballet Theatre

Cynthia Gregory

Ballet galas come and go, but only a few stay vividly in the mind. The Twentieth Anniversary Gala for Cynthia Gregory, staged by American Ballet Theatre (ABT) at the Metropolitan Opera in June of 1985 was such an event. Not only was it an evening charged with sentiment and glory, but for those close to the inner workings of the ballet world, it had its share of behind-the-scenes drama. Gregory's gala had been on the verge of being canceled, not by ABT, but by the ballerina herself, who, some 2 weeks earlier, had had a major confrontation with the company's director, Mikhail Baryshnikov, over her artistic future.

"I've always been quite outspoken when I believe in something," said Gregory, referring to the contretemps. "Without going into too much detail, it mainly had to do with my repertory for the next season. I want these last few years of my performing career to be exciting ones, to be creative ones, and to give me some real satisfaction.

"I want to feel that the 20 years I've danced with ABT have been worth it. What I was offered was unsatisfactory, and some heated words were exchanged. Finally, the air was cleared, although some things remained unresolved. It's true, the gala nearly didn't happen ... but in the end, I felt I should go through with it."

If Gregory's gala was fraught with undercurrents strongly affecting her professional life at ABT, a tragic factor in her personal life gave the evening an even greater sense of poignancy. Only 8 months prior to the gala, the ballerina's husband of 9 years, John Hemminger, died suddenly of a heart attack. This loss was commemorated in a program note that read: "Miss Gregory dedicates this evening to the memory of John Hemminger."

It is a tribute to Cynthia Gregory's great artistry and personal fortitude that her performances throughout ABT's spring season—an emotionally difficult one for her—contained a singular radiance, one that seemed propelled by some inner urgency, turning her every appearance into a memorable event. Indeed, the gala was the culmination of a season in which the ballerina had proven herself to be at the height of her powers, offering one dazzling performance after another, displaying both technical wizardry and interpretive depth, and placing her gifts in the service of an art she herself has helped to define and glorify.

Looking back on more than 20 years with ABT, Gregory claimed that in 1965, the year she joined the company, she had been in the right place at the right time.

"It was an exciting, thrilling time," she said. "A ballet boom was in progress, and the company had a fabulous repertoire. I entered as a member of the corps, although I had done leading roles with the San Francisco Ballet, my first company. But that was fine, because I learned so much! I mean, to see Carla Fracci and Erik Bruhn dancing together! To see Toni Lander and Lupe Serrano and Royes Fernandez ... to see Johnny Kriza in *Billy the Kid* or Sallie Wilson in *Fall River Legend* and *Pillar of Fire*! I saw all those great dancers and all those great performances—and they molded me.

"And it was a time when young choreographers were being developed—Michael Smuin, Dennis Nahat, Eliot Feld. And there were wonderful coaches, people like Dimitri Romanov, who was one of the greatest coaches I know. Also, when I joined ABT, they were doing just a few full-length ballets—*Giselle, La Sylphide, La Fille Mal Gardée*—but then came the *Swan Lakes,* the *Sleeping Beauties, the Coppélias,* the *Don Quixotes,* the *Nutcrackers* and the *Raymondas.* It was wonderful to be growing up as an artist in such an atmosphere.

"Very soon, I was given the opportunity of dancing in just about everything. Yes, some people thought I was too tall for *Giselle* and *Coppélia,* but I waited until I was artist enough to do them and to make people forget those extra few inches. So, maturing at ABT was a fabulous experience. Although there were some rough spots along the way, it's really been my whole life."

The "rough spots" Gregory referred to were the two times she resigned from the company, in 1975 and again in 1979. The ballerina was anxious to set the record straight on these dramatic departures.

"People said I quit ABT because of the many guest artists Lucia Chase was bringing into the company. That wasn't the reason at all. My only complaint was over the Russian defectors. You see, they had such fabulous built-in publicity; they were front-page news and became household names without even having to dance a step! Well, I said it wasn't fair that American dancers weren't being taken as seriously as Russians. I felt that we Americans were great dancers also and should be given just as much attention—that's all I ever said.

"Of course, there were other reasons I quit—personal ones. You see, I had had a lot of success and I was still quite young—just 29. Well, I couldn't handle things very well. I had no manager, no one to take care of me. I was dancing seven or eight times a week, always with a different partner. It got to be too much. Also, I was going through a divorce from Terry Orr. So, I just had to leave it all behind me and go away ... and I stayed away for a year.

"During that time, I met and married John Hemminger. He became my manager. When I decided to return to the company, John handled things for me, and I was less pressured, less frantic. In fact, I was very happy. As for the leaving in 1979, it was just for 6 months, and it was over a squabble about money ... something ridiculous like $200.00 per week. But that departure was good for me, because that's when I made guest appearances around the world, which was wonderful."

Gregory was reluctant to speak candidly about the current regime at ABT. All she would say about the Baryshnikov years is that the company had a more unified sense of style, that there was one vision at work, and that this was all to the good. "The depth of talent in the company is amazing," she said. "Ninety-some dancers, and not one clunker among them!"

What she *did* want to express was her particular joy over having become a friend to many of the younger company members.

"I feel I've become something of a symbol to them," she said. "It makes me feel so good that they know that I care about them. At first, I felt a bit alienated, because I used to think, 'Oh Gosh, I'm an old lady, and look at all those young dancers.' Also, I felt they would be afraid to speak to me. But now, I feel they appreciate me; they know that I'm *there* for them. That's a wonderful feeling! You see, I appreciate talent. I really do. It excites me. I never feel threatened. Even as a young ballerina, I never felt threatened by all the great dancers around me. That just pulled me up even more. I was inspired, and I think I danced better because of their presence."

Cynthia Gregory is aware that the passage of time takes its toll on any dancer.

"You just don't have the energy that you had before," she admits. "You have to conserve your energy. You have to be intelligent about the way you work. For example, I don't take class every day—at the most, three or four times a week. On the other days, I do my own barre—a slow warmup. I have a few more aches and pains when I wake up in the morning. I have to be sure that my rehearsals are placed in the right space of time during the day. I used to take things more for granted. Now, each performance really means a lot to me. I try to make each one of them very special—unique in its own way. I concentrate more ... because I know I only have a few years left to dance."

Clearly, it was painful for the ballerina to touch on the loss of her husband, John Hemminger, whose death was devastating.

"John was really my whole life," she said. "Most people might think that ballet was my whole life, but my life revolved around my husband. We were a team. We were the best of friends. We did everything together. I would have quit dancing for him at any moment. When he was gone, I realized that my dancing was what I had left. It was something I could fall back on to give me strength. Dancing helped me to hold on as I was trying to cope with everyday life.

"It's been difficult, but it's opened my eyes in a lot of ways. Some people might go into themselves, but I think I've come out of myself. I have developed more sympathy for people—more compassion. I see the world with new eyes. I realize how precious life is.

"I'll never forget John. His strength and his vision of me have kept me strong. He was a person who didn't believe in the trivial things in life. He believed in the overall picture. He made me believe in myself. He gave me the strength to understand myself as a person and as an artist. My love for him is still there, and always will be, no matter what happens to me."

In 1986, the ballerina remarried. In November, 1987, she and her husband, Hilary Miller, became the happy parents of Gregory's first child, a son, Lloyd Gregory Miller.

Lee Meddin

Photograph by Steve Speliotis

Lee Theodore

The sounds issuing from Studio A at New York's elegant Harkness House are wild. A combo of bongos and electric guitar is going loud and crazy. The music is a '60s frug, and the two young musicians at their instruments keep the beat steady, the rhythm even, and the drive of the tune staccato and soaring. Just what is happening in Studio A where classical ballet classes are usually held?

A look inside reveals that a class is indeed in progress, but the 16 young men and women standing in a group before the mirror are engaged in performing movements that don't resemble the *pliés* and *jêtés* of classical ballet. Leading the class is a tiny dynamo of a woman dressed in white slacks, blue top, and sneakers. Her eyes dart from student to student, and her voice follows in the insistent rhythm of the music.

"Five, six, seven, eight ... shake one shoulder, now the other ... head to the left, head to the right ... pivot and move back ... now straighten the torso, but keep the pelvis going ... pivot and come forward and repeat!" Some quick claps of her hands stop the class and the music. And Lee Theodore, who is conducting these proceedings, calls for a new rhythm from the combo in the corner. For an hour-and-a-half, the ongoing dance movements are carefully dissected and analyzed. Head, neck, shoulders, torso, arms, hips, and pelvis are given difficult and highly specialized isolated movements. When the group is ready, the movements are all put together, and, two by two, the dancers execute a perfectly coordinated variation that translates into an exhilarating '60s frug.

On other days, these same students learn the specific techniques and mechanics that will result in a '20s Charleston or tango, a '30s one-step, a '40s lindy or rhumba, or a '50s jitterbug or samba. Indeed, these classes offer a survey of popular dance styles set within a context of the American musical theater, and the whole range of these activities are only a part of the elaborate dance curriculum instituted by Lee Theodore, who in 1975, invented the American Dance Machine.

Far from being just another jazz-oriented company, The American Dance Machine is dance-historic, far-reaching, and visionary. Its goals, as set forth by Theodore, are aimed at reconstructing and preserving the best of American theater dance—the brilliant, show-stopping numbers of Broadway musicals choreographed by the likes of Jack Cole, Agnes de Mille, Jerome Robbins, Michael Kidd, and Bob Fosse, among others. All of these choreographers have devised dances that, through the years, have fallen into obscurity once a given musical has closed, flopped, or folded out of town. It is an attempt to give life and continuity to an art form that heretofore had been considered unworthy of preservation and relegated to nostalgic memory by a public that deemed the Broadway musical a light-hearted, albeit exciting and often thrilling, American phenomenon.

The American Dance Machine blossomed into a major dance concept, with important figures in the musical theater giving their unstinting support and with government assistance turning the project from dream to reality. Awarded substantial grants from the National Endowment for the Arts, the New York State Council on the Arts, foundations, and private donors, the American Dance Machine has established a wide-ranging program that will not only preserve American theater dance for future generations, but will provide qualified performers with professional training and instruction. The American Dance Machine also serves as a research center with a wide range of activities: selection of works to be reconstructed; compilation of individual histories of the works, memory sessions and rehearsals of these works; documentation through videotape and Labanotation; cataloguing and storing of theater-dance material in a permanent archive. First and foremost, however, the American Dance Machine is a "living archive"—a performing company of dancers that presents isolated dance numbers in their entirety, covering the spectrum of theater dance from the '20s to the present.

To understand the birth of the American Dance Machine, one must look to the person who dreamed it up. The diminutive and irresistibly energetic Lee Becker Theodore has long been a Broadway favorite and is perhaps best remembered as the original tough and poignant Anybodys in the Bernstein-Robbins-Sondheim 1957 smash *West Side Story.* She has also appeared in such musicals as *The King and I* and *Damn Yankees* and served as choreographer for *Baker Street, Flora, The Red Menace,* and *The Apple Tree,* among others. When *West Side Story* was successfully revived at Lincoln Center during the '60s, it was Lee Theodore who, at the invitation of Jerome Robbins, provided the original choreography and direction.

During a recent interview, Theodore gave some idea of her dizzying background and related the events that led to the formation of the American Dance Machine.

"I was born in New Jersey, and received a scholarship at the Swoboda School when I was 8-years-old. I worked with the Swobodas for most of my childhood. At 14, I came to New York and entered the High School of Performing Arts, where I received my modern dance training. I graduated at 16 and immediately started to work as a replacement in *Gentlemen Prefer Blondes.* After that, I joined the Slavenska-Franklin Ballet company and was also a guest artist with the Donald McKayle Dance Company and the New York City Ballet. At one point, I went into an Off-Broadway show called *Living the Life,* and it was during the run of that show that the producers of *West Side Story* invited me to audition for the part of Anybodys—which I got.

"But my life during those years was a madhouse! I mean, my schedule was studying with every teacher in New York—from Antony Tudor to Margaret Craske to Anatole Oboukhoff to Anatole Vilzak to Paul Draper. My schedule was rehearsing with Donald McKayle during my lunch hours, John Butler during my dinner hours, doing my Broadway show at night, my television shows during the day, and working on my own choreography between midnight and five in the morning. And it was grand and perfect!"

Immediately following the original run of *West Side Story,* in 1962, Lee Theodore was asked by the State Department's People-to-People program to create an evening of dance for the International Jazz Festival in Washington, DC. It led her to form her own small company, the Jazz Ballet Theatre in which she trained the dancer/choreographers Michael Bennett, Eliot Feld, Alan Johnson, Jay Norman, and Jaime Rogers.

"At the time, I had the idea that America needed a serious jazz dance company," Theodore said. "Essentially, what I did was to cover the spectrum of old jazz, new jazz, contemporary jazz and, at the heart of it all, improvisational jazz. I spent 4 months working with those incredible dancers who didn't even know that they would eventually emerge as fabulous choreographers in their own right. We worked, and we used live jazz musicians who were also improvising. There was an artist who did the sets by painting and drawing them, also in an improvisational manner—that was Paris Theodore, whom I subsequently married.

"Well, we had a fabulous time, working on a new concept of choreography. We performed in Washington and at the Boston Arts Festival, and it all lasted for about a year. Then, unfortunately—because I was too young to understand that a new idea needs planning, backing, and money—the company broke up. We disbanded, the boys went off, and for them, the rest was history. As for me, I decided to make a career for myself as a Broadway choreographer. I did *Baker Street, Flora, The Red Menace* with Liza Minnelli, and *The Apple Tree,* directed by Mike Nichols. I worked on several motion pictures. Ultimately, however, I felt that so much had been accomplished in choreography that it lacked humility to go into competition with Jerry Robbins, Jack Cole, Agnes de Mille, and all the other greats. I had to find a new direction, and the answer was becoming a full-fledged director."

Never one to do things by halves, Theodore plunged into an intense course of study in preparation for her newly chosen career. She became a member of the director's unit at the Actors Studio, and for 3 years studied acting with Alfred Ryder. Concurrently, she began work on original properties with playwrights and writers. She also became involved in children's theater, conceiving original children's musicals. For 2 years, she was director of Bill Baird's Puppet Theater. With unabating and boundless energy, Theodore lectured at universities, accepted teaching assignments, and staged musicals under the auspices of the New York State Council. It was also during this hectic period that the dancer/choreographer/director married Paris Theodore, and the two became the parents of two sons, Saïd and Ali.

Still, by 1972, she had had enough of the chase.

"I said to myself, where is it all leading? I'm running from job to job. It will all be over soon, and I'll be left with a handful of reviews and stories to tell my children. It was certainly not enough; my life would have to have more meaning. I felt I was being prepared for something more important. And it was at this point that I thought up the American Dance Machine. When the concept hit me, I knew that was *it*!

"It was May, 1972, and I was teaching at California State University, Long Beach. There was a critics' conference, and I talked about my little company, the Jazz Ballet Theatre. As I was talking, it occurred to me that my jazz theatre was really very limited in scope. How much better to preserve and save the best of theater dance, which incorporates jazz, by reconstructing it, preserving it, getting it put together, and establishing a company that is devoted to this kind of dancing. And I thought, 'What a wonderful idea? It's got everything in it that has meaning for my life.'

"I knew that what had to happen next was to make a feasibility study and so, between 1972 and 1975, I went around and asked a lot of questions: 'Can it be done?; Would the cultural community support such a project? Can I find people to reconstruct numbers that go back 40 years in time?' The general consensus was that it would be hard and tricky and that the question of snobbism would enter into it. Yes, classical ballets have been preserved and notated. Your *Giselles* and *Coppélias* and *Swan Lakes* have all been handed down. Graham and the modern dancers have found their niche in history. But what about theater dance? Nobody cares. Nobody has notated it. Nobody remembers it. It's plagiarized to death. Major choreographers like Cole, Robbins, de Mille, Fosse, and Kidd make their contributions and then second or third or fifth-rate people come in and imitate and copy it. Well, something had to be done. But I needed people who believed in this as strongly as I did, and I had to go out and find them.

"I talked to Gwen Verdon, and she said, 'Yes! It's about time!' Bob Fosse said, "Yes, that would be interesting. I'd like to see what you can do.' Agnes de Mille said, 'Absolutely! Documentation is the only way for choreographers to establish themselves as major artists! Everybody else has their stuff written down, scored, and notated, and they make money off it. We must do the same!' Oliver Smith thought it was a wonderful idea. Donald Brooks, the designer, said, 'Oh, what I wouldn't give to see those dances again!' Jerry Bock, the composer, said he would be glad to help.

"Then I ran into a very insightful person, George White, who runs the Eugene O'Neill Foundation. I explained my project to him and he was extremely responsive. He thought it would be beneficial to both our organizations if we came under the O'Neill Foundation auspices to get started. In this way, I could approach the National Endowment for the Arts for funding. Well, the Endowment was very visionary and came through with a major grant of $25,000.00 for 1976, which was our first year. I promised the Endowment a pilot program devoted to the theater dances of Jack Cole, one of the greatest innovators in the field. Now, I knew I was dealing with a choreographer who was no longer living. Yes, there were movies—*On the Riviera, The 'I Don't Care' Girl, Gentlemen Prefer Blondes, Designing Woman*—but they gave you style. I wanted to reconstruct actual numbers. Well, time ran out, and as it grew short, I decided to produce a film—a documentary on Jack Cole called *Recollections.*

"What I did was to gather together all the original Jack Cole dancers who would speak about him and remember him. I got people like Gwen Verdon, Buzz Miller, Florence Lessing, Beatrice Kraft, Bob Hamilton, Ethel Martin, and others. Everyone talked about Jack and what he meant to them and what he meant to theater dance in general. We included clips of his work in films. Along with the documentary, we hired eight dancers and put together a piece called *Vocabulary.* What was it? It was bits, pieces, snips, combinations, steps, and attitudes of Jack Cole. It was a statement of his style, and it firmly established in my mind that there must be a training facility attached to the American Dance Machine, because this kind of training is no longer available to the young dancer."

With the completion of the Jack Cole project, Theodore was ready for her next one which would be devoted to the reconstruction of dance numbers by Bob Fosse, Agnes de Mille, and Michael Kidd. Again, money was needed, and a second National Endowment grant came her way. This, like the first, was a matching grant of $25,000. To raise the matching money, Theodore prepared a series of reconstructed numbers performed at the American Theater Lab and at the John Drew Theater in East Hampton, Long Island.

We did the 'Quadrille' from *Can Can* by Michael Kidd. We did the 'Mute Girl Solo' from Kidd's *Finian's Rainbow.* We did the 'Whip Dance' from Kidd's *Destry Rides Again.* We put on dances from shows by Bob Fosse—'The Rich Man's Frug' number from *Sweet Charity,* and the 'Rich Kid's Rag' from *Little Me.*

"Well, the response was emotional. People were crying and laughing and applauding. And we raised $30,000.00 through solicitation following these showings. And it more than matched the grant.

How, precisely, does the American Dance Machine work? And how does it reconstruct its repertory?

"We go to the people who first did the original dances and who remember them. It's as simple as that. We call these people reconstructionists. On one number alone, there might be five or six of them, because what happens is that one person will come in and remember the first 16 bars, and the next person will remember what happened afterwards, and so on, down the line. Now, in some instances, some of these dancers have disappeared altogether. For example, I tried to find Anita Alvarez, who created the 'Mute Girl Solo' in *Finian's Rainbow,* back in 1947. I looked for her for nearly 4 years! Through an accident of fate, I discovered she was a farmer in New Jersey! Well, I got her phone number and called her. I said I wanted her to come in and remember her 'Mute Girl Solo' for us. She said, 'It's impossible! That was 30 years ago!' But she came in, and we started to play the music, and I could see her body moving and her head going, and within 3 hours she had gotten back the basic structure of the dance! It was beautiful. And the kids were sitting on the side watching and marveling that a woman her age still had all this mastery and artistry within her. Then, she began to tell anecdotes about the show, the choreographer, and how her number was created. I could see the kids' eyes grow as big as saucers, and I could see how hungry they were for that kind of information.

"The point is, there is no generation gap at the American Dance Machine, because we can work with a 60- or 70-year-old person and there's a connection—a lifeline. These people achieve a small piece of immortality by putting the dances they've created on a young dancer. That's the sort of thing that happens at The American Dance Machine."

A look at the training curriculum at the American Dance Machine makes more than clear that Theodore means business. The array of talent that gives courses of instruction is entirely extraordinary. A young dancer entering the American Dance Machine school must be prepared to audition in order to ensure placement in classes commensurate with their achievement level. But once admitted, these young dancers will be placed in contact with an altogether fabulous roster of theater professionals who will train them in every facet of theater dance and its allied disciplines.

As noted, Lee Theodore teaches 50 years of theater dance. On Mondays it's the '20s, Tuesday, the '30s, Wednesday, the '40s, Thursdays, the '50s, and Fridays the '60s. She demonstrates, gives basic exercises, and guides the young dancers through the styles of each era. She will talk about the choreographers who worked during those periods and place them in touch with the vocabulary of each major choreographer.

Nenette Charisse, a legendary name in the musical theater, has taught ballet—a first-rate ballet class in the strict classical tradition, but one which moves beyond ballet into areas of acting, space, expression, and expressiveness. Mme. Charisse has taught some of the greatest names in dance: Jerome Robbins, Michael Kidd, Pearl Lang, Valerie Bettis, José Limón, Gwen Verdon, Nora Kaye, Maria Karnilova, Mary Martin, Judy Holiday, Annabelle Lyon, and Tommy Tune, to name but a few.

Gwen Verdon has taught master classes in theater dance. Miss Verdon is, of course, a major Broadway star who appeared in *Chicago, Can-Can, Damn Yankees, New Girl in Town, Redhead,* and *Sweet Charity.* Says Theodore of Gwen Verdon: "She is the quintessence of the American Dance Machine. Within her body exists the art of Jack Cole, Bob Fosse, and Michael Kidd, all of whom have created works on her. She is a fabulous, fabulous teacher!"

Among other teachers who have been a part of the American Dance Machine staff are: Bick Goss, teaching cotillion, ballroom, and jazz dancing; Thomas Rosinsky, instructing groups in singing and vocal technique; Jack Lee, conducting workshops in vocal repertory; Peter Gennaro, the choreographer of *Annie;* and the venerable Agnes de Mille. Other courses have been offered in Aikido, ethnic dance, ballet, and even on how to audition.

Black theater dance and tap workshops have been led by Harold Cromer and Bernard Manners, members of the dance group "The Hoofers." Theodore says, "I'm trying to introduce something in tap that is not available in most commercial schools, and that's what I call Black Hoofing, which is a very old style of tap dancing. Why do I want to teach hoofing? It's because in our future reconstructions we are going to do numbers out of *The Blackbirds of 1922* through the '30s, the

Cotton Club Revues and Katherine Dunham. So, we have to train our 18-year-old kids how those dances were done."

Turning to the matter of the ongoing repertory, Theodore maintained that only theater-worthy numbers will be considered. "There is a lot of choreography that is not theater-worthy. Still, it should be catalogued, indexed, and put into an archive. But up until now, the candidate pieces for reconstruction reflect my own taste. Of course, everything is a question of feasibility. Some of the dancers who could remember certain numbers are not available to us. Other numbers can't be done, because our company is not ready for them.

"For instance, Bob Fosse won't give us permission to perform a number like 'There's Gotta Be Something Better Than This' from *Sweet Charity* unless we have three dynamite ladies to do it. Donald Saddler quite rightly claims that we don't have a mature enough person in our company to do the 'You Can Dance With Any Girl At All' number from *No, No, Nanette*. So, the specialty numbers are a real challenge to us.

Among the many contributions planned by the American Dance Machine is the protection of a choreographer's copyright.

"The copyright aspect is of major significance," said Theodore. "The general attitude of the choreographer, even outside of theater dance, has been that if they don't publish, they hold the copyright in perpetuity. The new copyright law admits video and film documentation as a publication, which means that choreographers can protect their work against plagiarism. They can also protect their initial contracts, if it says that the producer must make the first offer to revive the original choreography. Choreographers will not only have an accurate record of what their work looks like, but have proof that they did it. Therefore, the byproduct of our reconstructions has a great significance in establishing the copyrighted validity of the choreography in question."

As a performing group, the American Dance Machine is, indeed, a living archive, for it educates even as it entertains: "Our basic aim is to distill the dance. To show the choreography. We want to offer it in its purest form. We won't attempt to reproduce the look of the original numbers—the costumes—because that would prove extravagant for us. And we will not use the original sets and decor, but only the barest suggestion of what it was like, and then, only if it serves the choreography. If a number requires a stairway, a table, a platform, or a chair, for example, we'll use it. But basically, we're interested in the essentials—to show the inventiveness of the choreography."

For 20 years, the American Dance Machine achieved its goal of preserving Broadway dance in the living forum of the theater. Lee Theodore trained hundreds of dancers, documented many "lost" dances from the '20s through the '70s, and led her company on several nationwide and worldwide tours, carrying the message that Broadway dance is a serious art form. Then, in September of 1987, she succumbed to cancer after a long battle with the disease; she was 54-years-old. Although ill, she had continued to the time of her death fulfilling her role as Artistic Director, manager, teacher, and mentor. Today, the American Dance Machine has taken temporary quarters and is under the direction of Lee's husband, Paris Theodore. It is testimony both to the durability of American show dance, and the vision of one extraordinary dancer. Lee Theodore created a living archive of dance; it is up to future generations of dancers to continue her mission.

Photograph by Jack Vartoogian

Erik Bruhn

Erik Bruhn, who died on April 1, 1986, once said, 'The perfect dancer has not yet been born." This statement reflected both his humility and his sense of self-awareness. He realized that perfection is an abstraction—a goal, something ideal, perhaps something unattainable. And yet there is no question that for over 30 years Erik Bruhn represented the distillation of pure classical dance. As an artist he existed within a circumference of unmatched creative eloquence. No male dancer of his generation could approximate his singular gifts, and no male dancer since has risen to prominence without, somehow, having been touched or inspired by him. Bruhn transformed control into freedom. He transmuted technique into expressivity. Through his body the difficult became the inevitable, the complex became radiantly effortless. His was an all-giving vision of movement at its most exalted, and the art of male dancing in the 20th century was enriched by his presence.

What follows are quotes by Erik Bruhn culled from conversations I was privileged to have had with him during the writing of his biography, *Erik Bruhn: Danseur Noble.*

"If you don't have the confidence to show what you feel through technique, then you remain a product. Well, I learned to show more and more of my inner self and not to be introspective. In that way it seemed I became a bit more special in my relationship to the audience. I concentrated and I said, 'I'm not afraid of showing my feelings.' Of course, I *was* terrified, but I made myself come through—at least that human part of me that had a desire to dance. I felt that if you allowed *yourself* to come through, even within the form and discipline that was part of dancing, then you appealed to the imagination of the audience."

"You've got to hear the music for the first time every time you dance to it. If you hear the same thing every time, then you never feel the need to go back for *more.* The idea is that if you hear more, then you find more of yourself *in* the music. For me, music is a constant rediscovery."

"The reason I wanted to do the role of Jean in *Miss Julie* in the first place was to prove to the public that I could portray a dreadful and awful character. Actually, portraying such a role comes very easily to me, whereas being the noble prince did not come as naturally as people might suppose."

"There were times during my 20s when I wanted to stop dancing altogether. I remember, after having done 4 years of one-night stands with American Ballet Theatre, that I simply could not go on. Of course, it was hard on everybody, but there were moments when it got to be unbearable. Those one-night stands were simply not for me. But, in those years, that was the only way a company could survive. And when you do one-night stands, you also have them as a person—sexually. Believe me, I tried them, but they were so unfulfilling that in the end I stopped. I wanted full relationships, not in terms of years but in terms of intensity."

"I never tried to influence Rudik (Nureyev), but in a way he influenced me. He helped me through his incredible force and vitality. He was raw, and, of course, he was so young. I, on the other hand, being 10 years older, was merely polishing my technique. Yet, with all my acclaim of being the West's leading male dancer, I had reached a dead end. Seeing Rudik move was an enormous inspiration. It was through watching him that I could free myself and try to discover that looseness of his. Before Rudik, I had very little competition in the West, and it was only with Rudik's arrival on the scene that I really felt stimulated."

"To dance with Carla Fracci was to have fulfilled a love affair—a love affair consummated on the stage. Of course, I have had great satisfaction from dancing with other ballerinas, but this was something new. We did not recognize what we had when we first danced together in 1962. I mean, we met, we danced, we parted. But when we danced *Giselle* in Milan in 1963, we were both ready for what happened between us. The moment was there, and we were both prepared for it."

"There have been certain moments on the stage when I suddenly had a feeling of completeness. Even disguised as a dancer, I felt like a total being. This has happened perhaps four or five times during my entire dancing career. It was a feeling of *I am.* At those moments, I had that indescribable sensation of being everywhere and nowhere. I had the sense of being universal ... but not in any specific form. It was that very same sensation that helped me to pull through the toughest periods of my life."

"We who work on the stage have a tendency to contemplate our navels—to be totally self-involved. At the same time, we are supposed to be all-giving. Many artists think that *whatever* they do is good enough for anybody. Of course, this is a terrible fallacy. A balance has to be reached. And that balance is a combination of dream and reality. One of my major struggles has been to retain my sense of reality as an artist, because I knew that if I were only living a dream then I would lose contact with the real world."

"What people don't understand is that my so-called moodiness and my desire to be alone usually occur at times when I am in the process of replenishing myself as a human being. They have seemed to make me a man of mystery. They are qualities that have, at times, disturbed my relationships with others. For example, love affairs have been disturbed or stopped because the other person did not understand this need for solitary renewal. They felt that I was not sharing something with them, that I was keeping things from them. But they were wrong. What I was trying to do was to keep myself sane."

"I don't fall in love with love. When love is offered to me, I do not always respond well. I do not like for love to be something possessive. I find it smothering. For me, loving does not mean owning. Of course, one wants a response. Sometimes there is none. There were times when I fell in love, and I was not loved back. But I do not regret having felt something for someone. It's not that I am of the school that says it is better to give than to receive. But at least when I loved someone the emotion was valuable. It is important to love. We all need to give love and to receive love. I was privileged to have had at least a few affairs that were mutually satisfying. Those that failed were when someone tried to possess me. *That* I could never abide, and when a relationship turned in that direction, it became destructive. It burned me out as a person and as a dancer."

"I never wanted just to move *through* life but rather to go deeply into it, even at the cost of complete personal fulfillment. If I have left some small mark in my profession, then I am content. But what ultimately means most to me is having matured as a man and perhaps reached some sort of inner strength to keep me alive and alert to everything and everyone around me."

Photograph courtesy of Columbia Pictures Entertainment, Inc.

Ann Miller

When Ann Miller finally made her entrance in the revival of *Sugar Babies*—a long 20 minutes into the show—the theater went wild. It's as if a collective memory had stirred and awakened ... the vision had materialized and there she *really* was—*all* of her—the jet-black lacquered wig, the pert porcelain face, the insouciant smile, the gorgeous long legs, and that ineffable something that spelled total stardom. Yes, Ann Miller was definitely, without a question, you'd better believe it, make no mistake about it, *there*!

And when she started to tap-tap-tap, flicking her hands and flashing her smile and throwing those looks ... well, the house went crazy all over again, because it wasn't just Ann Miller in *Sugar Babies* up there, it was Ann Miller in all those low-budget, late-night B-movies of the '30s and '40s and '50s for RKO, Republic, Columbia, and MGM—oldies but goodies with cute titles like *Reveille with Beverly, What's Buzzin' Cousin, Eve Knew Her Apples, Thrill of Brazil,* and *Watch the Birdie.*

If Ann Miller was "Queen of the Bs" for nearly 3 decades, grinding out picture after picture of less than memorable quality, it wasn't for lack of trying to be way up there with Judy, Ava, Rita, or Lana ... or even Mickey Rooney! It was just that Ann Miller wasn't all that tough or maybe all that ambitious. She didn't bitch and holler the way some did, didn't have agents hustling for her ... maybe didn't have the luck. Even later on, when some good parts came her way in movies like *Easter Parade, On the Town,* or *Kiss Me Kate,* the roles were secondary. It was Kathryn Grayson, never Ann, who got the man. For Ann, it was strictly second-fiddle time.

But second fiddle or not, Ann Miller emerged a star and a big one at that, the kind that transcends mere nostalgia. Having put in her time in nightclubs, in movies, on stage, on endless TV talk shows, having even tasted Broadway glory as the fourth *Mame* in 1969, Ann Miller landed on her feet with aplomb, elegance, and wit. With Mickey Rooney in *Sugar Babies,* she romped through tacky-wacky burlesque skits with endearing breeziness and low-down charm. When she sang, it was with heart and gusto, and when she tapped, the audience was completely hers.

Meeting Ann Miller in person isn't just meeting a star, it's confronting a legend. Lunching with her is not just sharing a meal, it's an event. Said lunch took place at swank "21" and it wasn't your quiet, cozy *tête-a-tête.* Miss Miller enjoys the company of men, and, as it turned out, four of us sat dazzled as Ann Miller, in expensive green silk, made chit-chat an art.

Of course, almost everyone as "21" knew Ann Miller was in their midst, and admiring glances came from all directions—as well they might. For a woman of a certain age, Miss Miller looked radiant. Slender, with that perfect complexion and ageless mien, she offered the image of iridescent well-being. As talk progressed, it soon became clear that Ann Miller, for all her endearingly ditzy front, is a person of depth and guilelessness. Born in Texas, she evinced the Texan's love of grit and honesty—that down-to-earth, plain-talking sense of what's what and what's real.

Touching base with her past, she first spoke of her late mother. "Mother was like bread—a staple. She was the anchor. A wonderful woman! She was not a stage mother. My going on the stage was a matter of having to eat. You see, mother and dad divorced, and mother took me to LA from Houston. She was very hard of hearing and couldn't seem to hold down a job because of it. When dad started cutting off the money—he wanted us to come back to Texas—I started to take little jobs dancing at the Elks Club and the Rotary Club in LA. I was only 11, but I knew how to tap and I guess I was kind of cute, and that's what kept us going. Then, I entered an amateur contest at the Orpheum Theater and won first prize. The manager gave me 2 weeks of work at the theater. Some agents came, and I landed a job at a nightclub called Casanova. Some people saw me there, and engaged me for the Bal Tabarin in San Francisco, where I worked for 16 weeks. One night, Lucille Ball walked in with Benny Rubin, who was a talent scout for RKO, and Benny offered me a contract. The next night, Columbia Pictures walked in, and *they* offered me a contract. It didn't rain, it poured, and that's how Ann Miller was born!"

When Ann Miller turned 15, she had completed 3 years of work at RKO, appearing in such films as *New Faces of 1937, The Life of the Party,* and the classic *Stage Door,* in which Ann played an aspiring young actress opposite Katharine Hepburn, Ginger Rogers, and Lucille Ball.

"It was fun being in the movies and part of Hollywood, and my career was on its way. While I was still only 15, I had the chance of going to New York to appear in George White's *Scandals of 1939,* and I was a big, big hit. I only had two tap numbers, but I made a splash all over the New York papers with color spreads in the *Daily News* and the *Daily Mirror.* So, having made this big splash in New York, I went back to RKO and my salary shot up from $150 a week to $3,000 a week, which was a lot of money in those days. Well, I made more pictures at

RKO and then went to Republic and made a couple of movies there, one with Gene Autrey, in which I gave him his first screen kiss.

Finally, I went to Columbia and stayed for 6 years. Harry Cohn was my boss, and he was good to me. I never saw the ugly, mean side of him that I had heard so much about. After that, I went over to MGM—and it was Mecca. It was the Ziegfeld of all the musical studios, and that was wonderful, except I never really got that one great part I had dreamed about … it just never happened. In the end, MGM started to fall apart, and it seemed Hollywood more or less collapsed. It was the beginning of the end of that fabulous golden age—the end of a great, great era."

Ann Miller, with her perky looks, her snappy delivery, and her 500-taps-a-minute talent, could look back on a film career that found her portraying endless chorus girls with a heart of gold—the sweet-tough "other woman" who invariably lost out.

"I had a long career, but never really became a top star like Judy Garland or any other number of ladies. You see, I was always very even-tempered, which was part of my problem. Mother would always say, 'Isn't it wonderful that you have this glorious contract and that everybody just loves you so!' But I probably should have fought harder for bigger and better parts. As it was, I did things as they were dealt out to me, and, finally, my MGM contract just ebbed out, and they didn't resign me, because they weren't resigning anybody."

By the mid-'50s, Ann Miller had turned to television and to the musical theater. She appeared in various segments of popular TV shows, and crossed the country starring in such productions as *Can-Can, Hello, Dolly!, Panama Hattie, Blithe Spirit,* and *Glad Tidings,* all of which culminated in her Broadway appearance as *Mame,* the smash Jerry Herman musical.

"I hadn't been on Broadway for 30 years, and Jerry Herman had seen me doing *Mame* down in Florida. So he brought me to Broadway. The show was ready to close, but when I took it over, it continued to run for almost a year. I finally had my big chance even though it was a hand-me-down. It still wasn't my own show—it was really Angela Lansbury's show. It took Harry Rigby to dream up *Sugar Babies,* and I had no idea the show would be such a big hit. We all thought it would be this dark horse. To be absolutely frank about it, it still isn't what I really want. I would like to be in a show like a *Mame* or a *Dolly*—a story that's built for me, because, believe it or not, mine is still a career that's budding! I mean, the stage is a whole new window for me."

Throughout her life, Ann Miller has had any number of rich and powerful admirers. Men such as Conrad Hilton, Howard Hughes, and Louis B. Mayer offered her entry into the heady world of unlimited wealth and glamour. But Miss Miller claims that these were not romances, but solid friendships. As for love, it brought her more pain than she cares to remember. As it turned out, she had the distinction of having married not one, not two, but three millionaires. All three marriages added up to a scant 5 years of what Miss Miller describes as wedded torture.

"At the tail end of my contract with Columbia, in 1946, I married a fellow named Reese Milner of Consolidated Steel, and it was a disaster. My boss, Harry Cohn, begged me not to marry him, because he knew of a couple of girls Milner had been mixed up with, and he treated them very badly. I could hardly believe the stories! But when I married him, I found out they were true. Well, we had a baby, but it died, and the marriage collapsed after only 1 year. Then I waited for about 12 years before I married again, this time to a fellow called William Moss, who was from Texas. It lasted 3 years, and it didn't work out either. So, after my divorce from Moss, I married a man called Arthur Cameron, but he was not a well man. There was always something wrong with him ... and *that* marriage lasted about a year.

"All these men promised me the moon. They were all wealthy. Each time I got married, I gave up my career, because they didn't want me to have one. I became their hostess, their show horse, and all the things these people seemed to need in their lives. The trouble is, when you marry playboys ... well, most of them drink and like pretty girls, and I was not about to be one among 15 girls! My last husband just loved his mistresses—wouldn't give up any of his girls. I said, 'Either they go or I go.' He said, 'Pack your bag!' So, I went back to my career. You see, I thought I was in love each time I married, but when you find out they had other pussycats on the side ... that's not right. They wanted to keep me and still have their fun, and I didn't want to play like that. To me, that wasn't nice. I don't like fun and games—that's not my style.

"You see, I'm not really as spaced-out as people think. There's a side to me that's very serious. When I fell in love, I fell in love for keeps. But if something goes wrong, you don't want to prolong the agony. It's like shoes that hurt. And you don't want to wear shoes that hurt. So, these things hurt me and I just got out of them. No, I'm not in love now. Oh, I have people I love and like, but there's no big love in my life."

Smiling wistfully, Ann Miller added, "Thank God for the sweet, kind fellows who care for me. I tell you, these boys have just kept me and my career going. It's just incredible. Believe me, I find them just so sensitive and kind and loving. I think they're the sweetest people in the world. They're like brothers to me—really wonderful. They take my interest at heart ... worry about me. I just love them!"

How does Ann Miller see herself?

"Well, I'm an Aries—born April 12—but I have Taurus rising, which makes me a very *definite* person. The Bull and the Ram, you know! If I have to make a decision, I make it and that's *it.* I guess you'd call me a perfectionist. In a way, I'm like a German drill sergeant. Take *Sugar Babies.* When I walked in and found something wasn't right in the show, everybody knew it. If the chorus boys didn't do this or the girls didn't do that or somebody missed a line, *boom* goes a note. I want things to run like clockwork. So, that's one part of me.

"Another part of me? Well, I had four seers tell me that I was an Egyptian queen in another lifetime—Queen Hatshepsut, about whom very little is known. I've been to Egypt four times, and the people at Luxor took me to see Hatschepsut's tomb. Whenever I stood in the middle of her temple, I felt things ... vibrations that made me feel I had lived there before. It was eerie! I've often thought how awful it would be if five or six other people had been told they were Queen Hatscheput, and we'd all be stuck in the same room together. What a hoot *that* would be! But I love Egypt ... everytime I left Luxor, I just cried."

Even as Ann Miller brilliantly toiled in *Sugar Babies,* her eye was on the future. Since leaving the show in 1986, she has hosted the Academy Awards and appeared on various television programs, including a segment of *Love Boat,* in which she costarred with Ethel Merman, Carol Channing, and Della Reese. Now, all that's needed is that hoped for smash hit Broadway musical that will announce once and for all that Ann Miller, erstwhile 'Queen of the Bs," is a superstar with a glittering capital S!

Peter Spalling

Photograph by John R. Johnsen; Courtesy of Martha Graham Company

Peter Sparling

Martha Graham is a mythic sorceress who has long known how to shape the hearts and minds of her dancers. She does it with the force of her genius—with an uncanny combination of insight, love, cruelty, and spirituality. Dancers become her instruments, her subjects, sometimes her toys. Her dancers either rise to her ecstatic level, or they are broken and perish.

Peter Sparling, a Graham dancer since 1973, has quietly risen to her visionary plateau, offering performances of radiant and seamless authority. His strong, taut, compact body moves fearlessly within the Graham universe, smoothing itself around the contours of a vocabulary he has made his own.

To have seen Sparling dancing leading roles in *Dialogue, The Plain of Prayer, Part Real-Part Dream, Diversion of Angels, Appalachian Spring,* and *Acts of Light* was to be in touch with an artist who had gone deeply into himself and emerged victorious over an aesthetic that broaches no false move, no superficial posturing, no inner hesitation. With something approximating blind fervor, he placed his art in the service of Graham's stern and luminous voice, extracting from it a resonance and clarity that gave each dance its own truth.

Sparling does not have the heroic bearing favored by Graham. He is slighter, more poetic, more thoughtful. His deep-set eyes and ready smile conjure a softer version of the Graham male. His strength lies within a churning inner passion that is unleashed on stage. In person he seems mild, understated, secretive. But there are rumblings pushing to get out.

"Martha has taught me that there are certain drives that remain with us always, that can't be ignored. She has taught me that if one has a passion for life, one mustn't be afraid to express it. But she has also taught me the value of holding on to a certain remoteness, a certain aloneness that enables you to observe—to take things in. I have learned that part of being a creative person is accepting that remoteness, that aloneness."

Peter Sparling has always been a precocious loner. The second of six children, he was born in Detroit, Michigan on June 4, 1951. His mother and father are musicians—she a singer, he a pianist. From the first, the youngster had strong ideas about what he wanted to do. At the age of 8, he insisted on being given dancing lessons. As the only boy in an all-girl class, he soon mastered the Sailor's Hornpipe. It was a beginning, but the dancing only lasted 6 months. In public school another interest beckoned: the violin. Offered instrumental training, he fell in love with the fiddle and for the next 9 years, playing it was his all-consuming passion. So serious was Sparling about his chosen instrument that he resolved to become a concert violinist. To that end, he spent the last 3 years of high school at the Interlochen Arts Academy in Michigan.

"I had gone to music camp at Interlochen when I was in junior high school and just fell in love with the place—that beautiful setting in the north woods! When the Academy offered me a scholarship to continue my studies, I jumped at the chance. I had very intensive musical training and became principal second violinist in the Academy orchestra. But during that 10th-grade year, I also decided to take a course called *Introduction to Dance.* I took it to fulfill my physical education requirement. Well, I loved it so much that by the end of that year I said, '*This* is what I want to do!' I was magnetized by dance."

Sparling was 16 when he fully switched to dance at Interlochen. Coming under the tutelage of William Hug, who had created the dance department, he immersed himself in the techniques of Humphrey, Graham, and Limón, that were fostered by Hug. There were ballet classes as well, but the modern techniques were Sparling's primary studies—and he soon excelled in them. Throughout his rigorous 2-year apprenticeship, the young dancer also began to experiment with choreography. He was particularly intrigued with the work of Merce Cunningham, whose book, *Changes: Notes on Choreography,* became something of a bible. His earliest dances were based on "chance" occurrences, a hallmark of Cunningham's choreographic technique.

"I was off on my own Cunningham head-trip," he says. "My dream, of course, was to come to New York and join the Cunningham company—but it never happened. Somehow, I needed the umbrella of a school, a home base. And so I applied and was accepted at Juilliard. There, my principal teachers were José Limón, Helen McGehee, Ethel Winter, and Bertram Ross. It was an incredible education."

Sparling remained at Juilliard for 4 years. He was awarded the Louis Horst Memorial Scholarship and earned his BFA degree in 1973. As it turned out, Juilliard was the launching pad for his earliest success as a dancer and his first encounter with Martha Graham.

"Helen McGehee and Ethel Winter taught a group of us *Diversion of Angels* for a Juilliard performance," Sparling remembers. "They wanted to have Martha's approval, and we all took a crosstown bus to see her and to perform for her. I recall entering that strange shrine of a building in the East Sixties, where Martha's school is located. And there she sat, looking very remote, but with very bright eyes—razor-sharp eyes that zeroed in on absolutely everything. We performed—I was in the *Couple in Red*—and when it was over we all sat at her feet, and she said, 'Well, you men looked pretty good. *But you women!!*' And she cut into them and shocked the hell out of those poor girls. She gave them her classic gambit of 'Where does the dance come from?' and they were just terrified. But finally, she gave us her blessings and we performed the piece. So that was my first version of Martha.

"But my first professional work came with José Limón. José had asked me to join his company in 1971—I was in my third year at Juilliard—and it was my first taste of working with a major company. We did a lot of touring, and I had the opportunity of working very closely with José. José was mesmerizing. He was the strongest presence of a male dancer that I had ever seen. He epitomized the nobility, pride, and physical strength of the male in dance. His musicality was so poignant and touching! His sense of theater came through his musicality—very different from Martha's. Martha's sense of theater comes through the timing—the visceral timing of the muscles—that contract-release thing, where the dancer speaks a constant inner dialogue *against* the music, but *with* the music, too. It's what causes the electricity in her works.

"With José it was different. He immersed himself totally in the music and came out riding it. He was suspended in its net—caught in it! For José, the music was all. And it was wonderful dancing his works. I remember our driving out to his farm in New Jersey and rehearsing one of his last works—*Carlota*. I danced the role of Maximilian, and he rehearsed us in his converted barn. One night, I slept in the barn in my sleeping bag. Something woke me up. It was José. It was the middle of the night, and José was in the barn pacing back and forth, back and forth. You see, he knew he was dying—and he had to finish *Carlota*. I didn't dare disturb him. Well, that year, 1972, we were on tour in Hawaii without him. And we received a telegram saying José had died in New Jersey."

While Peter Sparling was performing with the Limón company in 1972, he received an invitation from Bertram Ross to join the apprentice group of the Graham company. It would be Sparling's entrée into the next phase of his career. Soon after Limón's death, Ron Protas, Graham's associate director, asking Sparling to become a member of the Graham company.

"I came in just at the crossroads," recalls the dancer. "It was the summer of 1973, and after a long absence, Martha had come back to head her company that spring. I was of the generation that also saw Peggy Lyman, Tim Wingerd, and Janet Eilber coming into the company. Another dancer, who joined the following year, was Shelley Washington. I had known Shelley during my Interlochen years—that's where we met. Well, when the company was on its Asian tour, Shelley and I became engaged, and we were married in 1974. The following year Shelley left Graham to join Twyla Tharp's company, and we lived in very separate worlds. The marriage fell apart. We were just too young to weather the storms. After 3 years, we divorced."

Sparling was clearly experiencing the tumult of living, dancing, growing, and finding himself. And working with Martha Graham—being in her constant orbit—proved a lesson in survival.

"One of the problems was that I kept myself too remote. It was partly my fear of confronting all those demons that Martha brings out in you. It was Martha's mission to unlock them—and I resisted. Martha saw my talent. She saw my musicality. She also knew she had to pull things out of me. So we fought. We fought in subtle ways. She trusted me with a lot of her new pieces, but not with the old ones—her big classics. She gave me leads in *Holy Jungle, Scarlet Letter, Plain of Prayer,* and *Shadows and Frescoes.* She would speak to me about dancing too much in my head. She said I had to physicalize the dancing—that I couldn't be subservient to the music, that I had to be on top of it and to project. But I was afraid of asserting myself.

"You see, she felt that we all hold in ourselves this seed of utter physicality. She wanted us to come alive at every moment through absolute commitment in our bodies so that our musicality and spirituality would just flow out. The trouble was, I had always approached her dances from a very intellectual point of view. So it was a gradual process of relinquishing this remote position and diving head first into her repertory—into whatever it meant to be Hyppolitus in *Phaedre* or Orestes in *Clytemnestra.* It was a psychological process—of knowing what it *meant* to be those characters. Well, after years and years I learned that lesson, but it was a struggle."

Sparling danced with Graham for 6 years, maturing in his roles, mastering his technique, refining his interpretations, submitting himself to Graham's exhortations to abandon his reserve and to go fully and bravely into her dances. Concurrently, his talents as a choreographer began to blossom. Throughout his years with Graham, he would work independently, creating works of considerable strength and originality. During the times the company was off, he would give solo concerts, some attended by Graham herself. She would appear backstage complimenting him, giving him courage to continue. Finally, in 1979, Sparling felt he needed to make a break. He needed to be on his own. He was forging a career as a choreographer, and the impulse was to form his own small company. He told Graham he needed to leave. Graham understood.

"At first, I formed something called 'Peter Sparling Presents Solo

Flight.' Then I formed the Peter Sparling Dance Company. I was also a founding member of the Ann Arbor Dance Works, which is the University of Michigan's resident dance company. In the middle of all that, I traveled to Portugal to stage works for the Ballet Gulbenkian and at the Cloud Gate Dance Theatre in Taiwan. I would also return to the Graham company to do an occasional New York season. It was a crazy time. Of course, I tried to keep my own company going. We gave consecutive seasons at the Riverside Dance Festival, and I choreographed like mad—three premieres every year!

"Well, this all lasted until 1983, and it got to be too much. I was the director, the choreographer, the dancer, the fundraiser, the PR man, as well as the teacher. I realized that the point of all this was being lost. So, tired of the struggle and lacking significant financial backing, I just gave up. I disbanded my company. What I learned from all this was that independence was a curse as well as a blessing. And it was wonderful to rejoin Martha's company where you didn't have to worry about bookings, rehearsal schedules, and funding. I could reimmerse myself in my roles and feel free just to soar on stage."

But Sparling's innate need for independence soon reasserted itself. After completing a season with Graham, he accepted an invitation from Robert Cohan to spend a year in London teaching at the London Contemporary Dance Theatre. It was an unhappy experience. ("They wanted someone to pamper the dancers, and I just couldn't do that.") By 1984 he was back in the States. That same year he became an Assistant Professor in the dance department of the University of Michigan, a post that allows him to continue performing with Graham; in the fall of 1987, Sparling was appointed Chairman of the University of Michigan's dance department. Each year Sparling rejoins Graham for her New York seasons.

Today, Peter Sparling has moved into a new maturity. Most telling is his enduring dedication to Graham, whom he has poignantly watched moving into her own great maturity. Indeed, the character of his dancing seems to have progressed and developed in direct proportion to Graham's own extraordinary journey into old age. Sparling speaks movingly of Graham still creating in her 90s:

"Martha is always battling with her own powers and energies. Sometimes, in her studio, her mind wanders, but she knows when that happens and she'll say, "I can't work anymore.' Or 'I can't *think.*' And she'll stop. Her process of doing new works is interesting. As long as she has time to let things ferment, to gather up a lot of material, she can arrange and bring a work together. She can work an entire week on 30 seconds of a dance—changing it, driving the dancers crazy, doing over and over again the same section until she's comfortable with it.

"Martha chooses principals who have done her repertory—who have done a significant range of roles—to forge a character in her new works. She doesn't move around. She sits in her chair in the studio. She comes in 2 hours in the afternoon, and then returns in the evening for an hour and a half. She will play the music she's interested in over and over again. Often, she'll throw it out in disgust and frustration and try a new score. The dancers stand by. Some will stand in the back trying out steps. Of course, she sees everything, and she'll say, 'What did you do just then? Come and show me.' She'll take the step, then add to it, saying, 'Do a tilt to the side and a split-leap to the floor.' She directs verbally with that shared vocabulary.

"So she uses the dancers, and she has staff around her—Linda Hodes, her associate artistic director, Bert Terborgh, the company rehearsal director, and his assistant, David Hochoy. They all sit by Martha and act as interpreters. Ron Protas will wander in, and he'll egg Martha on. Martha has entrusted Ron to be her *provocateur*—someone she can work against. She seems to need that. Martha can still be very bitter and can come out with scathing criticisms. But then, she'll turn around and tell a story that will make light of everything. Basically, Martha sits there watching the action. You see her dabbling with a very formal architecture on the stage—with symmetry, with arrangement, with formal groupings. And the fire is still there—you just sense it."

Although Sparling's career as dancer is burgeoning, he is more than aware of the passage of time. He can also look back on a life inextricably woven to his great mentors—Limón and Graham—and reflect on his own sense of being.

"I can see parallel lines that merge and then part again in my personal life and in my career. I have had a series of extremely painful and then extremely ecstatic exposures. I tend to leave myself open to experiences that overwhelm me and from which I must recover—pulling in, becoming remote, and putting the pieces back together again. I hope that some day it won't be such a struggle—that there won't be such extremes.

"As for my dancing, it's a very, very delicate process being able onstage to peel open all those layers that you cover your heart with. But you do it, because there is a context—a flow—a beginning, middle, and end that you can trust. There is a sense of beauty that is retained, and a poetry that makes you survive. It's just so rewarding tapping that source in Martha's works, because it allows the poetry to flow—you just *resonate* with it! What I'm working on is letting my personal life flow into my creative life. I suppose it's hopeless. I suppose artists have spent their entire lives struggling with that conflict. But I've got to search for that resolution. Maybe I'll find it. Maybe I won't."

Rudolf Nureyev

Photograph by Linda Vartoogian

Rudolf Nureyev

The Nureyev image is larger than life.

No one who has seen him dance can ever forget him. No one who was danced with him has remained unaltered. No one who has come into his personal orbit has remained indifferent to him. As artist and personality, Nureyev is an emblematic figure whose drive and power has changed the face of dance and whose presence in the world of Western ballet has provided a generation of male dancers with a new *raison d'être.*

If Balanchine claimed that "ballet is woman," Nureyev has irrevocably placed man at her side, insisting, through conviction and example, that he is her equal, if not her dominant partner. His impact on dance in general has been so potent that he has given it a new lease on life, investing the art with a new sense of daring, excitement, and glamour. Single-handedly, and with incalculable effect, he brought dance into the consciousness of a world-wide public—from the man in the street to the ballet specialist.

The Nureyev legend began on June 17, 1961, at Le Bourget Airport in Paris, when his so-called leap to freedom instantly made him the best known dancer in the world. He had appeared with the Kirov Ballet at the Paris Opéra when he took his decisive step. It was the first major defection of a Soviet dancer to the West, and it commanded international headlines. Indeed, the publicity surrounding Nureyev's defection was staggering. Everywhere he went, he was followed, photographed, and interviewed. It was perhaps the first instance since the advent of Nijinsky in which a ballet dancer engaged the imagination of a worldwide public.

Almost immediately, he was invited to dance with the Paris-based Grand Ballet de Marquis de Cuevas. He became an overnight sensation. Ballet cognoscenti pounced on the Soviet dancer and quickly took note of his formidable gifts—his blazing stage persona, his thrilling, pantherlike leaps, his breathtaking elevation, his dizzying turns. They also noted his more than occasional lack of polish. Still, there was no doubt that Rudolf Nureyev, at age 23, had arrived.

Cut off from his past, Nureyev literally molded himself into an indefatigable pursuer of artistic excellence, a model for the male dancer, a ballet star of the first magnitude. With relentless fervor, he set about deepening his artistry by working with the best coaches and teachers Europe had to offer—he had already absorbed the great lessons of his Leningrad-Kirov mentor, Alexander Pushkin—and he began to follow a vision that would place him in the forefront of international dance.

To see Nureyev at his peak was to be in the presence of theatrical fire. From the moment he stepped on stage, audiences were literally spellbound by those elusive components that placed them in a dream state. Even as their critical faculties were open to assess a given performance, a subtly paralyzing effect caused them to rivet their attention upon a creature who seemed himself possessed.

The fact is, in his greatest performances, Nureyev was gripped by demons both benign and evil—demons that goaded and propelled him into action, into movement, into the flames of vulnerability and exposure. Strangely enough, the stage seemed an unnatural milieu to him. It was closer to a battlefield—an arena of combat and conflict that repeatedly needed to be conquered.

Nureyev once said, "Being on stage is really very abnormal. There is something very artificial about it. Because I feel so alien on the stage, I have a need to be on it more and more and more. But once on it, I am lost. It's like a sacrifice—and I give of myself completely. The moment I'm on stage, things become multiplied and magnified. It's like having an atom reactor inside of me. There is a chain reaction and, suddenly, my whole body bursts into flames."

Indeed, during his best years, the vision of Nureyev was a compelling mixture of suppressed fear and dazzling abandon, of muted desperation and unabashed ecstasy. And, always, there was his great and mysterious artistry. During the course of a ballet, supreme self-awareness was matched in equal measure to total immersion in role-playing. The more vivid a characterization, the greater Nureyev's own image appeared burnished upon it. The two were inextricable, for Nureyev imposed himself on any role he undertook. If we believed his Albrecht, Siegfried, or Romeo—and we unswervingly *believed*—then we also knew that it was Nureyev's own charged being that gave us entry into this belief. On stage, Nureyev was always Nureyev. It would never be otherwise.

In 1962, this most unique and explosive of Russian dancers met the coolest, most collected of British ballerinas—Margot Fonteyn. The two formed a partnership that blended gold and silver to mesmerizing effect. It was Ninette de Valois, then the director of London's Royal Ballet, who invited Nureyev to join the company as a permanent guest artist and to partner Fonteyn in the company's production of *Giselle*. The date of this historic performance was February 21, 1962. For ballet lovers, lightning had struck not once, but twice within the span of a year. Not only had Nureyev established his own charismatic presence in the ballet world, but in consort with Fonteyn, had formed what has been deemed the greatest ballet partnership since Vaslav Nijinsky and Tamara Karsavina.

At the time, Fonteyn was 42. Nureyev was 18 years her junior. And yet, the combination produced a stunning oneness that has yet to be equaled. Fonteyn, nearing the end of her career, had miraculously regained her strength and vitality, offering performances of consummate, translucent beauty. Nureyev, for his part, acquired a new-found depth—an ardor and humanity that transformed an already electrifying dancer into a noble one. Indeed, it was the Fonteyn/Nureyev partnership that turned the Soviet star into the ultimate romantic *danseur*, for, in the light of Fonteyn's maturity, he inevitably assumed the guise of a gallant, impetuous, reckless lover.

This chemistry, this mutual awareness, this uncanny harmony between two dancers of dramatically disparate backgrounds and sensibility, would last some 17 years and would find undiminished glory in some 26 roles, varying from full-length classics to brief duets. Nureyev said of the partnership, "When I dance with Margot, there is one aim, there is one vision. It is painful arriving at that vision, but when we have found it, we go there together. There is no tearing us apart."

Nureyev's American debut did not take place on a ballet stage, but on television. He replaced an ailing Erik Bruhn in a performance of Bournonville's *Flower Festival Pas de Deux* on *The Bell Telephone Hour* produced in 1962. His ballerina was Maria Tallchief. This single television appearance (and subsequent guest spots on *The Telephone Hour* and the *Ed Sullivan Show*) projected his image to a nationwide audience, and his super stardom in America was assured.

Nureyev's first appearance on an American stage took place on March 10, 1962, when, as a guest artist with Ruth Page's Chicago Opera Ballet, he partnered Sonia Arova in the *Don Quixote Pas de Deux* at the Brooklyn Academy of Music. His enthralling virtuosity brought the audience to its feet, and New York's ballet intelligentsia had a field day dissecting his virtues and faults. Finally, everyone had to admit that Nureyev was not simply a presence, he was a force.

What has to be understood about this quixotic artist is that along with his unquenchable thirst for the dancing experience ("If I don't dance, I crumble"), he has always been someone who needed to immerse himself fully into every facet of his profession. To that end, and very early on, he began to produce his own versions of the classics (*La Bayadère* ["The Kingdom of the Shades"], *The Nutcracker, Don Quixote, Raymonda, The Sleeping Beauty,* and *Swan Lake*), as well as original choreography (*Tancredi, Romeo and Juliet, Manfred, The Tempest,* among other works).

Moreover, his interest and curiosity in dance styles other than classical ballet found him studying modern dance techniques and eagerly performing in the works of modern choreographers such as José Limón, Glen Tetley, Paul Taylor, Martha Graham, and Murray Louis. Nureyev dared to do it all. Mostly, however, his repertory in the West encompassed some of the greatest names in the 20th-century choreography: Mikhail Fokine, George Balanchine, Frederick Ashton, Kenneth MacMillan, Maurice Béjart, Rolard Petit, Jerome Robbins, John Neumeier and Birgit Cullberg. In every instance, he heightened the psychological intonation of their works through performances that resounded with intensity.

Apart from his genius as a dancer, Nureyev's fame continues to rest on the myth of his personality. By his own admission, he has always been a man alone. "Wherever I go, I am an intruder," he once said. Solitary, moody, vulnerable, and suspicious, he moves through life bearing the scars of a difficult, poverty-stricken childhood—he was born on a train journey between Lake Baikal and Irkutsk on March 17, 1938—and a less than happy adolescence spent in search of proper ballet training. Finally, at the age of 17, he was accepted in the Vaganova Institute for Choreography, the famous school of the Kirov Ballet in Leningrad. Here, his superiors found him too awkward, erratic, and frequently insubordinate. Slowly, however, and principally through his tutelage and friendship with Alexander Pushkin, Nureyev, the dancer, was born.

Still, his rebellious spirit prevailed, and in the West his unpredictable temperament came to the fore. Stories abound of Nureyev's tantrums. One witnessed, read, or heard about scuffles in backstage corridors, dishes smashed at parties, insults hurled at fellow dancers, and ballerinas slapped. There were tirades against the press, critics, managers, conductors. There were hints of anti-Semitism. Whether exaggerated or not, this less than attractive behavior revealed the underside of Nureyev's flailing raw energy. His bursts of temperament, often superbly staged and impeccably timed, were grist for the publicity mills. Not since Maria Callas, the great opera star, had an artist used the media with greater cunning or theatricality.

The pressures of Nureyev's life, his nonstop dancing schedule, his global commitments, and, above all, his steely discipline, leave him little time for close personal attachments. Still, there are enduring, loyal friendships and many displays of generosity. If Nureyev can cut someone to the quick, he can also be a lesson in charm and friendliness. If he is difficult to work with, he can also be unstintingly helpful to his fellow artists. Sullenness can alternate with impish, wry humor, rudeness with solicitude. Nureyev, at his best, is a man obsessed with excellence and perfection. In the working situation, adherence to these ideals is paramount. Artistic truth, as he sees it, lies in the upholding of tradition leavened by imagination and creative zeal. Anything less arouses his ire and contempt.

Nureyev's thirst for the new and challenging is boundless. Wherever he goes, he seeks it out. In whichever part of the world he finds himself, he goes to pains to attend concerts, art exhibitions, films, and dance events that might enrich his spirit and nourish his curiosity. And the more avant-garde an event, the better. Nothing gives him greater pleasure than to spot new talent or to discover aspects of creativity that might quicken his imagination.

As a wealthy and glamorous figure, Nureyev likes to live accordingly. He maintains homes in Monte Carlo, London, Paris, and New York. He owns a farm in Virginia. His current domicile in Paris is designed to house a prince. When traveling, Nureyev indulges his taste for luxurious hotel suites and classic restaurants. Postperformance sorties find him in chic night spots accompanied by an entourage of the rich and famous. Dressed in the latest fashions, Nureyev is the constant center of attention. This "solitary intruder" is no stranger to the sophisticated ways of the world, and he moves in it with *panache* and aplomb.

In 1983, at the age or 45, Nureyev was appointed Artistic Director of the Paris Opéra Ballet. It seemed inevitable that the dazzling Charles Garnier palace should become the setting and seat of one of the world's most dazzling dance personalities. Unlike several of his predecessors, Nureyev did not bend and bow to the unwieldy machinations that have burdened the Paris Opéra House for centuries. With characteristic single-mindedness he began sweeping away the cobwebs and turning the company into one of the most prestigious in the world. Within months of his appointment, he provided his heretofore spoiled and somewhat somnolent dancers with new incentives. Inviting choreographers as diverse as Karole Armitage, Lucinda Childs, Andrew de Groat, Nils Christe, David Bintley, and Michael Clark to create new works for the company, he has provided his artists with fresh and challenging choreographic points of view. In addition, the company now performs the works of Antony Tudor, Paul Taylor, Rudi van Danzig, and Ivo Cramer, among other contemporary masters. Indeed, in the short years of his tenure, he has transformed the Paris Opéra Ballet into a technically brilliant and forward-looking ensemble.

Today, Rudolf Nureyev has emerged as more than a legendary dancer, more than a visionary company director, more than a world-renowned figure in the arts. He is history personified. The century that spawned him will always be remembered as having contained his unique and radiant presence—one that illuminated all of dance, enriching its tradition, and, in many ways, assuring its future.

Photograph Courtesy of Patricia Bowman

Patricia Bowman

In a sense, great ballerinas never die. Some don't even fade away. Anna Pavlova, for one, is still alive in the minds of millions and her memory is a living, palpable thing. Of course, Pavlova was Pavlova—a genius unto herself. No dancer has ever duplicated her myth, nor entered the world's collective unconscious.

How presumptuous to infringe upon an image that, through the years, has become magnified to a point of sacrosanct indelibility. How daring, perhaps, to speak about an American ballerina in the same breath as the Russian goddess of dance. And yet, the time has come to risk the analogy, not in a spirit of comparison—Pavlova was incomparable—but within a context of "She might had been ... if only!"

The American ballerina in question has now fallen into obscurity. At the time of this interview, she lived quietly in midtown Manhattan, her only companion, an aging poodle. When there *were* ballet pupils, she instructed them with care and brilliance. But the pupils were very few, and mostly, her days were spent in solitude in the smallest room of her sizable apartment—a sitting room, noted for its meager bow to taste or elegance. And yet, this inconspicuous setting came to sudden life by the presence of a woman whom critics have called the American Pavlova.

Her name: Patricia Bowman.

Is it possible that we have forgotten Patricia Bowman, our first contemporary American prima ballerina? Perhaps we have grown too blasé over a dance explosion that has produced innumerable American artists of stature. Perhaps, in our quest for the latest, newest, and most exciting, we have allowed our memories to be shrouded by veils that have long obscured those dancers who have given the American public its first glimpse of memorable native talent. If so, it is time those veils were lifted, so that we might recall and rediscover the singular art of at least one dancer still in our midst whose artistic maturity coincided with a moment in our dance history when her art could not find its proper setting.

Prior to 1930, classical training grounds in America were relatively scarce. American youngsters, eager to make ballet their life, had virtually no opportunity to establish important individual careers. Even as they flocked to the schools and studios of the newly arrived émigrés, hoping one day to emulate an Anna Pavlova or a Vaslav Nijinsky, and even as they followed in the most arduous and refined methods of classical training, the opportunities for practicing their craft were practically nonexistent. A lucky few could enter an opera company's corps de ballet or be given a solo. Others might attempt a ballet recital, which would draw scant audiences and even scanter press coverage. The fact was that there were no American ballet companies to join. Indeed, during the '20s, classical dancing was, for the most part, relegated to "specialty numbers" that would find "toe-dancers" appearing in vaudeville, musical comedy, night clubs or popular extravaganzas such as George White's *Scandals* or the Ziegfeld *Follies.* There were a few other outlets, such as stage presentations that accompanied a first-run motion picture. These movie palace variety bills, featuring singers, comics, dog acts, ventriloquists, et cetera, would also include dancers whose training might have merited a far more auspicious setting. In short, dancers with first-class ballet training behind them could only be showcased in show biz.

Bowman was one such artist. She rose to stardom under performing conditions that all too often undermined a talent that, under different circumstances, in a different land, or in a different age, might far sooner have placed her in the front ranks of classical dance. As it turned out, Bowman did achieve the status of prima ballerina in America, but the road to such eminence was paved with countless setbacks, frustrations, humiliations, and iron-willed endurance.

"I was born in Washington, DC, but I'm going to keep the year a secret! My background is English-Irish, although both my parents were born in this country. My father was a manager of sorts. Mostly we lived in hotels. My mother always wanted to be on the stage, but her parents wouldn't allow it, and so she vowed that if she ever had daughters, she would let them go on the stage if they wanted to. I have a sister, Marie, 3 years and 3 months older than I am. We both have red hair. At the time, we thought, 'How awful!' *Nobody* had red hair then. I didn't mind it when I grew up. My father never wanted me to dance. My mother, on the other hand, was *always* behind me. Father said 'No,' but mother had her way.

"Because we always lived in hotels during my formative years, I never had the right foods. I was always very nervous and emotional. Mother thought that if I took some dancing lessons, it would do me some good. My father claimed that my mother was killing me, because I was too fragile. But the dancing lessons came through. There was no technique in those days. It was the Irish Jig or the Sailor's Hornpipe, or the minuet. I adored it all. When I turned 7, I studied with one of the best teachers in Washington. Still, there was no barre and no real technique. It was just a little bit of dancing ... a bit of hopping around, you know. Mother thought I was pretty good. One day, she saw a newspaper advertisement, announcing that Paul Tchernikoff would be the balletmaster of the Washington Opera Company.

"Now, Paul Tchernikoff was really an American from Boston, who had Russianized his name, because he had danced in Pavlova's company. Also in the company was a lovely lady by the name of Lisa Gardiner. Paul Techernikoff and Lisa Gardiner went into partnership and opened a school together. They also danced together with the Washington Opera. I applied for a job in the ballet corps of the opera company and was accepted. At the time, I was about 9. I danced in *Samson and Delilah,* and John Charles Thomas sang in it. So that was my professional debut. Then, I took real ballet lessons from Tchernikoff and Gardiner, and it was the *best* training! I worked with them for about a year and a half.

"My next appearance came about through a quarrel between Tchernikoff and Gardiner. For some reason, Lisa got terribly angry with Paul and refused to partner him in *Aida.* So he said, 'All right! I'll dance with Patsy Bowman!' I was 10-and-a-half. We did an adagio together, and I remember that President and Mrs. Coolidge were in the audience. Well, that was an exciting night. Then, Paul Tchernikoff decided to stop teaching and to stop dancing. He went off to a whole new life. But I went on with my studies with Gardiner, and, little by little, gained some real technique.

"And so, I performed with the Washington Opera and I studied with Miss Gardiner and also attended regular school. When I turned 15, a woman by the name of Albertina Rush came to Washington with a big show of dancers. She was also recruiting dancers for George White's *Scandals* in New York. I auditioned for her at the RKO Theater in Washington, and she accepted me. The only problem was, how to tell daddy? My father kept arguing with my mother. He'd say, 'How do you know she's going to be better than anybody else? I'm spending all this money on her lessons! How do you know she'll make it in New York?' Well, mother believed in me, and said, '*I'll* pay for her lessons!' And she did. She went out and worked just to pay for my lessons. She worked as a milliner in a department store in Washington. And I worked, too. I used to pose for painters in my little ballet costumes. I would sit for hours and hours, and I'd put the money away for toe shoes.

"In the end, mother and I left for New York. I dropped out of school for good, because I was going into George White's *Scandals*! I had a 32-bar solo, and I danced in the ballet corps and in all the chorus numbers. I worked so hard! And I began to earn some money.

"In New York, I studied with a woman by the name of La Sylph. She used to be a big dancer on the Broadway boards. She had one bad eye, and she didn't cover it with a patch. I went to her because she was very cheap. When she saw what I could do, she told me I was too good for her—that she couldn't teach me anything. She said, 'Why don't you go to Fokine. He's the best.' I told her I couldn't afford anyone like that. But La Sylph had read in the papers that Fokine had formed a small ballet company and would be doing performances at Lewisohn Stadium. La Sylph thought I should go and ask if I could join the company. Well, I thought I'd try. I remember La Sylph telling me, 'Be sure to tell Fokine I sent you!'

"Mr. Fokine and his wife, Vera Fokina, who was a famous ballerina in the Serge Diaghilev company [the Ballets Russes], lived in a gray-stone mansion at 4 Riverside Drive, near 72nd Street. I rang the bell, and a butler came to the door. Fokine *always* had the butler open the door. I told him I wanted to see Mr. Fokine. He said, 'Does he know you?' I said, 'No." Right in back of him stood Fokine. He came up to me and said, 'What is it you want?' I said, 'I'd like to apply for a job.' And then I told him that La Sylph had sent me. 'Never heard of her,' said Fokine.

"So then, Mr. Fokine said, 'You'll have to audition for me.' And he told me to come back the next day. When I auditioned, I did all my fireworks—fouettés, beats, pirouettes—everything. Oh, I was trying to be as brilliant as I could, and Fokine said, 'That's very good! But can you run?' Well, I looked at him in surprise. I was almost insulted. I said, 'Of course I can run!' 'Well,' he said, 'if you can run, let me see you run.' I felt embarrassed. I said, 'Run where?' And he told me to run around the room. He said, 'Run as though there were a wind in back of you.' So I ran fast and I ran slow. I had my toeshoes on. Fokine watched me and said, 'You're very good, but you don't know how to run.' And with that, he took off like lightening, and he ran around the room twice. He was up on his toes, and his chest was back and his head was back. He ran without faltering. He was gaited in precise rhythmic patterns. It was the most beautiful thing I'd ever seen!

"I was hired to dance in his company, which would be performing at the Lewisohn Stadium in New York. He was the premier danseur and Fokina was the ballerina. He choreographed *Medusa, Les Elves,* and *Russian Toys.* That was the program. I was given an adagio in *Les Elves* and as my partner, Fokine wanted to get a boy by the name of Nicholas Daks. Now, Daks was the premier danseur at the Strand Movie Theater. He didn't need the money, and he didn't need the job. But he agreed to dance on the condition that I would be his partner. 'I want to dance with the redhead, or I won't do it!' he told Fokine. So, we were a pair together.

"We opened at the Lewisohn Stadium on a hot July night. I had never seen such a big place in my life, and I had never seen so many musicians in my life. We had this big symphony orchestra. I was scared to death. I remember that after one of the rehearsals, I went home and got terribly sick. I went to bed. I upchucked. I had a fever. It was because of stage fright. I couldn't stand that big, vast, open-air place. I really thought I wouldn't be able to go through with it. Finally, I did what I had to do. As a matter of fact, I did 16 fouettés. I also looked up at the stars, and that sort of made everything all right.

"After that performance, Mr. Fokine took us on tour. When we returned to New York, I got a call to go back into the George White's *Scandals*—which I did. You see, Fokine's season was over, and I had to work and earn some money so that I could pay for my lessons with Mr. Fokine. He was expensive—$5.00 per lesson—and I could only afford to take two lessons a week. But Mr. Fokine was so kind! He agreed to give me an additional lesson per week, free of charge. So I worked three times a week with Fokine.

"To study with Fokine was a joy and thrill, and, of course, ultimately, I fell desperately in love with him. It was the kind of thing that if he even shook my hand or touched me, I didn't want to take a bath for a week. It was like that. Of course, I had to keep it to myself. It was real love, but I couldn't let on, because if I did, Fokina would have banished me, which happened to some of the other girls in the school. Fokina was a very jealous woman!

"Anyway, there was a ritual about working with Fokine. As I said, he lived in this beautiful mansion. You walked up about four steps, you rang the bell, and the butler opened the door. You entered a marble vestibule. Just beyond was a very ornate living room. There were big paintings on the walls, which were done by Fokine himself. He was a wonderful painter. The pictures were of himself and of Fokina in various roles. In the back was the dining room, and in the center, there was a marble staircase. At the top of it was a multicolored skylight. At the foot of it was a desk, with an open book in which you signed your name. There was a tiny elevator, and a man would take you up to the fifth floor, which was sort of an attic. It was very bare—only a couple of chairs and a small mirror. That's where you changed. There were no hangers, so you put your clothes on the floor, or over the chairs.

"To take your lessons, you went down the back stairs, which was a very dark spiral staircase. So you groped your way down to the fourth floor. There was a tiny studio that had a big fireplace, a mirror, and barres. Everybody went to their favorite place at the barre. There was no room for me, so I went to the fireplace, and held on to it. After that, the fireplace was always my spot. In a while, Fokine came to this fourth-floor studio and gave a barre. There was no music, just him clapping or singing or stomping on the floor with his cane. He gave such a hard barre! You really had to come early to warm up, or you couldn't do it.

"He taught in degrees of percentages. He'd say, 'Your leg is only 35 percent. Could I have maybe 65?' Or he'd say, 'That's 50 percent. Can I have 75?' He'd say, 'That's very good, but could I have 100 percent?' These lessons would last about half an hour, and then we'd all go down through the third floor, which was the Fokines' private quarters, and on down to the second floor, which was the big ballroom of the mansion. It had ivory-colored walls, trimmed in gold, with little cupids all around the ceiling. It had a fireplace, and there were big French windows which looked over the Hudson River. You could hear the foghorns. It was a marvelous, eerie, beautiful, exciting place.

"Fokine had no pianist, except very occasionally, and he had no recordings. So, he would sing: 'Dah, dah, dum, dum, yum, pah, pah, pum, pum!' He'd sing everything. Or he'd count. You had to be very technical in those classes. Fokine did not take beginners—only advanced students. In this ballroom, we learned parts of his repertoire. I learned the boys' parts of *Prince Igor.* The jumps. And I learned the arm movements in *Schéhérazade.* And we did *Les Sylphides,* from the Mazurka to the Prelude to the Waltz. So, I became well-versed in these famous Fokine solos. And that's what we learned. Then, he'd let us practice on our own.

"One time, I stayed longer than the rest. I didn't want to leave. You see, I was *so* in love with him. I just stood there, after everyone had gone, and there was Fokine, playing the piano. He played so beautifully! He was composing something. He was a wonderful composer, and he was working on a beautiful composition. Well, I just stood there listening. Suddenly, he looked up and saw me. He stood up and bowed to me. Naturally, I felt very flustered and quickly rushed out of the house.

"I went on working with Fokine, but I had to continue earning a living. By this time, my father had gotten sick and had come to live with me and my mother. It was now the late '20s. I danced here and there—in vaudeville, small revues, anything I could get. It was a rat race. During that period, they had famous ballroom couples, like Velaz and Yolanda, Fowler and Tamara, and the Dancing De Marcos. Well, Tony De Marco had seen me dance and, just then, he was splitting up with his partner, Renée. He asked me if I would take Renée's place. Well, I'd never done any ballroom dancing before, but I thought I'd give it a try. I worked with him for about 6 weeks, learning ballroom dancing. Tony would take me to the Hotel Ambassador in New York, just to dance—just so we could get to know each other on the dance floor.

You see, ballroom dancing has a very special technique. Your foot has to be spaced just so on the turns.

"Finally, Tony and I went out on the road, just to try me out. We went all over the place, appearing in clubs and in vaudeville. I did all my routines perfectly, and Tony saw I was ready for New York. We opened at the Academy of Music down on 14th Street. And the next place was The Palace—The Palace Theater! That was the big time. We were headliners.

"This should have been one of the happiest times in my life, but it wasn't. You see, Tony wanted me to do solo numbers on pointe, while he went back to change. He sort of worked me to death. We'd come out, and do our first number, then, I'd have to change into a tutu and toe shoes and do a solo. Then, I'd have to change back to another costume and do a fast fox trot with Tony. Well, it got to be so bad that I developed an infection in one of my toes. It was just too much. Still, looking back on it, it was a great experience, although I didn't want to do any ballroom dancing for 2 years after that!

"Around 1929, I received a call from Nicholas Daks, who was a headliner at the Strand Theater, and with whom I had danced at the Lewisohn Stadium with the Fokine Ballet. Daks wanted me to be his partner at the Strand, which was a movie house. There would be a movie; then the stage show would start, and there would be all sorts of acts. Comics would come out, do their stuff, and then introduce us as the famous 'Tootsie-Dancers.' They'd get up on their toes and make fun of us. It just made me boil! Anyway, Daks and I did little ballets. One of them was called *Artist's Life.* I was a painting and he was the artist. I would come to life, and we'd do a pas de deux, and then I'd go back to being a painting, and the scene would fade out. I got my first review in *Variety* while I was at the Stand. They called us 'hoofers,' because they knew nothing of ballet.

"At one point, Daks was asked to come to the Roxy Theater, and, again, he wanted me along. That's how I got into the Roxy, which was a very big place—very classy. So, we went in, and we did lots of ballets. We did *La Gioconda* and *The Music Box* and a version of *La Sylphide.* I became a big star at the Roxy. I guess it was because I did things nobody had ever seen before in such a place. For example, when we did *La Sylphide,* I did fouettés diagonally across the stage, which really stopped the show. *Nobody* had ever seen that before, and I had never done it before either. Well, that really secured the Roxy for me. I became their ballerina, and I danced there for over 3 years.

"Then they brought in Léonide Massine in 1927 to stage ballets and to dance in them. Massine came to the Roxy with his wife, who was known as Eugenia Delarova. She was a soloist and also danced in the corps. When there were important character parts, she would dance them. The first thing Massine did was "The Blue Bird" pas de deux from *Sleeping Beauty*. He and I danced that four times a day! Now, at the real ballet, the girl who gets to dance "The Blue Bird" just does it once and is used for nothing else during the evening. But at the Roxy, they had four shows a day, and we danced that pas de deux four times every single day for weeks! To this day, I hate "The Blue Bird." I hate it with a passion! Still, that was the time when my name went up in lights for the very first time. It said, 'Leonide Massine and Patsy Bowman'!

"Of course, it was a thrill to work and dance with Massine. I mean, he was very famous and had danced with Diaghilev, and he was an important choreographer. But, to be honest about it, I found him to be a very cold person. He had these big brown eyes and when he looked at you, it was as though a cow were looking at you. You know, he would just stare right through you. Anyway, we danced together for 2 years.

"But he used to make me so mad. He'd be working with me, and he'd always say, 'Choura did this, and Choura did that.' He was, of course, referring to Alexandra Danilova, who had danced in his ballets. Well, Massine always made me follow what Choura had done. Later, when I met Danilova, I jokingly told her I hated her, because Massine kept referring to her all the time. She was very funny, because she said, 'You know, when Massine came back to Europe, after working with you at the Roxy, he kept saying to *me*, "Patsy did this and Patsy did that!" So, I hate you too!' But Massine was a worker, and I learned a lot.

"And so, I worked at the Roxy Theater and got to be a big star there.

"While I was dancing at the Roxy, I fell desperately in love with Mr. Rothafel—Roxy Rothafel. Oh, God I was in love! I guess it was the father image, because he was so much older than I was. When Rothafel opened the Radio City Music Hall, he wanted me as his ballerina. But I was really exhausted at that point. I decided I'd take a vacation in Europe; the Music Hall hadn't quite opened yet. So, I went to London and while there studied with Nicholas Legat. Then, I went to Paris and studied with Lubov Egorova. Then, I went to Berlin and studied at the Wigman School with Margarethe Wallmann. Working with Wallmann put me to bed for 2 days. The technique just undid me. I couldn't walk after I got out of those lessons.

"When I returned to New York, I went straight back to Mr. Fokine, because he was my most important teacher. By this time, I could afford to take private lessons with him. He had many private pupils, including Betty Bruce, Paul Haakon, and Orest Sergievsky, and we all became friends.

"Anyway, I opened the Radio City Music Hall. We had a big line-up of stars that first night. There was Ray Bolger and Harald Kreutzberg and lots of other well-known names. It rained cats and dogs that opening night, but the evening was a big success. Although Leonidoff produced and supervised all the stage productions at the Music Hall, I did a lot of solo numbers which I brought in myself. It was during this period that Fokine created several numbers just for me. He also taught me 'The Dying Swan', which he had choreographed for Pavlova—and that was a funny story.

"I knew that nobody had ever done 'The Dying Swan' except Pavlova and Vera Fokina. But I wanted very much to do it, and so I asked him to teach it to me. Fokine said, 'I will have to ask Madame Fokina's permission, because I've only taught it to one person other than Madame, and that was Pavlova. Madame won't have anybody else doing it, unless we ask her permission.' Well, Fokina was very nice about it. She condescended to let me learn it—for a fee of $300.00. After I had learned it and paid him all that money, he showed me a book containing all the steps for 'The Dying Swan.' *There* were all the pictures and all the positions. Well, if you were musical and really smart, you would have been able to learn that dance just by studying that book. Anyway, after he taught me 'The Dying Swan,' he said, 'Here, take this book. You might forget some of the steps, and they're all in here.' Then he made me pay an additional $5.00 for the book!

"Fokine also created two works just for me. One was called *The Persian Angel,* which had music by Mussorgsky and Glinka. Fokine designed my costume as well, and it was spectacular. It had these large wings and I wore Persian pants. The story of the ballet is about this celestial creature, who longed to enjoy earthly things. I did this wild dancing toward the end, and my wings became detached, and then my crown, and I danced and danced, consumed by earthly passion—and then, I danced myself to death.

"Mother traveled with me everywhere, and she thought that *The Persian Angel* was too classical for the audiences I was playing to. Since there were no real ballet companies to join, she thought I should make my life in musical comedy, and should get together numbers that could show off my versatility. So, that's when Mr. Fokine created that second ballet for me. It was quite contemporary, and it was called *Tennis.* He went out on Sundays to watch the tennis players on Riverside Drive. As a result, the dance was very authentic and very inventive. I wore a little tennis tunic—the sort that Billie Jean King wears today. And I had a visor, with a red and white bow. I had a tennis racquet. The whole number was about serves and picking up the ball and throwing it—just like a tennis game. So, I did a lot of galloping and running around the stage. It was a 4-minute number, and that's a lot of dancing for one person alone. But whenever I danced *Tennis,* it was always a big hit.

"When Mikhail Mordkin started his ballet company, it was Lucia Chase, one of his pupils, who put up all the money. As I understand it, they formed the company in 1937 and went out on tour, with Lucia Chase as their prima ballerina. Well, it proved a dismal flop. At the time, the company was handled by Columbia Management, and they refused to send them out again, unless the company could find another ballerina—someone with a name. They didn't want Lucia as the ballerina. So, a man by the name of Richard Pleasant came to me, because, at the time, I was a big star. He asked me if I'd be interested in joining the Mordkin Ballet as prima ballerina. I said yes, because, frankly, I wanted to get away from all that hectic jazz I was up to. Mr. Pleasant talked to Lucia Chase, but she thought I would be too tall—that there would never be the right boy to partner me. Well, I *did* look long. I had long legs, but I was only 5-feet, 2-1/4 inches. Anyway, Lucia kept saying 'No.' Mr. Pleasant kept insisting, and, finally, she said, 'Let Mordkin decide.'

"I was taken to meet Mordkin. I remember he was just starting a class, and I was invited to watch him teach. Well, he just about scared me to death. He behaved like a madman. I mean, his outfit alone! He wore these black tights and white sneakers and a pajama top. And he had a stick, and he went around the room singing and ranting and raving. He looked completely nuts—crackers! I didn't think I could *ever* work with anybody like that. In fact, I saw no sense in even sticking around. I just picked myself up and left the classroom without even meeting him.

"The next day Mr. Pleasant called, and he tried to get me to come back. He explained that Mordkin was behaving in that way, because he was sort of showing off before me. He was putting on a performance and cracking the whip and giving those kids a hard time. But what I saw was just a mess. Anyway, Pleasant was quite insistent, and, finally, I agreed to come back and meet Mordkin. This time, he didn't act up at all. In fact, I really liked him, and, finally, came to love him—not like Fokine, of course, but as a real friend. And so, I joined the company as prima ballerina. They didn't pay you much, certainly not what I had been used to getting. But I was in a real ballet company, and it would be steady work. I was so happy, because I didn't have to pay for my own costumes, orchestration, and publicity.

"The company was very good. Of course, there was Lucia Chase, and she put up the money, and she danced. There was Nina Stroganova, Leon Varkas, Dimitri Romanoff, Karen Conrad and Edward Caton. Sergei Soudekine did sets and costumes. The president and managing director was Rudolf Orthwine. We had a good repertory. We did *Giselle, La Fille Mal Gardée, Swan Lake,* and Mordkin's *Trepak, The Goldfish, Dionysus,* and *Voices of Spring,* which he did just for me.

"I remember Lucia Chase taking the company to her summer home in Naragansett, Rhode Island. We stayed in her house, and we rehearsed in a big clubhouse nearby, which she had bought for that purpose. What a different life it was up there! I was given a big room, all to myself, and a maid would bring breakfast on a tray. There I was, like a lady, sitting up, with breakfast in bed! Then, we'd be driven by car to the clubhouse for our rehearsals. Well, it was like a fairy tale. After rehearsals, we'd go to the beach, and lunch would be served. Then, we'd go back to rehearsal, and then we'd be driven back to the big house, where we would all come down to a gorgeous dinner and champagne, served by a butler. Lucia was very generous. And it was a marvelous way to learn one's roles!

"The Mordkin Ballet went out on the road, and we had fantastic success. We went everywhere—up to Nova Scotia, Toronto, Quebec. We went all around Pennsylvania and Ohio. And we danced in burlesque houses, and in other places that were smelly and awful. But we were a big success. Then, Lucia decided to play a whole week in New York—at the Alvin Theater on Broadway. We sold out! Then we danced at the Hudson Theater on Sunday nights, and, again, we sold out. It was fantastic.

"In 1940, Lucia Chase decided on a big change. The Mordkin Ballet got to be Ballet Theatre. She got a lot of dancers and choreographers from Europe. She got Anton Dolin, Antony Tudor, Hugh Laing, Andrée Howard and a lot of other people. And she formed all these 'wings.' There was an American Wing and a Russian Wing and an English Wing. She brought in Fokine to set *Les Sylphides.* Well, poor old Mordkin's nose was out of joint. And mine too—almost. She called the company Ballet Theatre, and I was still there, but from that time on, things started to go downhill between me and Lucia. They decided to put the dancer's names in alphabetical order. Well, that was OK, because I was still first, since there wasn't anybody whose name started with A. But then, they wouldn't let you know when you were going to dance. That was really mean, because you couldn't plan ahead. They'd be rehearsing three ballerinas for *Giselle* and four ballerinas for *Swan Lake,* and you didn't know who was going to do it. You found out only one day in advance.

"Well, that created bad feelings, because friends of mine wanted to know when I was going to dance, and they couldn't find out. It was one thing after another. I got into awful fights. I fought for what I had built up, and they were tearing me down, together with a lot of other people. It got to be a big company, and it was a worthy company but ... I had had my name up in lights!

"Still, I continued to dance with them. Dolin created a wonderful jazz ballet called *Quintet.* I had a wonderful role in that. But Lucia hated it. I remember, we shared a dressing room, and just before I went on in *Quintet,* she said, 'I have never, in my whole life, put on such a bad ballet. I don't know *why* I ever consented to do it. I just can't stand it! I know it's going to be a terrible flop!' You see, it was her way of putting me down. But *Quintet* got all the reviews. It was a smash!

"I stayed with Ballet Theatre for 1 year. I left because I was desperately unhappy. I just couldn't go on with it. So, I simply left."

After leaving Ballet Theatre, Bowman continued to perform for another 15 years in regional ballet companies, including the Chicago Opera Ballet and the St. Louis Civic Opera Ballet, and at Radio City Music Hall, on Broadway, and throughout the country in special guest appearances. She even had her own television program on the New York CBS station for 13 weeks in 1951. However, she never again enjoyed the security of working permanently with a single ballet company.

In 1955, after her father died, Bowman decided it was time to settle down. The constant demands of touring had worn her down. Her mother, who was still living with Bowman and directing her career, suggested that the dancer open a ballet school. Using her apartment as her base, Bowman kept the school going for over 20 years, although in later years students were few and far between.

Patricia Bowman summed up her life with a note of wistfulness: "I guess I've had a wonderful life. But, you know, I've always been alone. I've never married. You see, I was never in one place long enough. Of course, mother was always with me, but then she died— that was some years ago. Now I'm even more alone." This situation was remedied in 1977, when Bowman wed a long-time friend in Las Vegas. Sadly, her husband died soon thereafter, and Bowman was left a widow. She continues to teach privately and appears as an actress in productions in Las Vegas.

Michael Bennett

Michael Bennett and Donna McKechnie
Photograph by Jack Vartoogian

Michael Bennett

To watch Michael Bennett put together a show-stopping number, such as the closing of Act I of *Dream Girls,* was to be in the presence of a wily craftsman whose understanding of pacing, form, and structure was only second to his instinctive grasp of show biz razzmatazz. As the three gorgeous black girls of the show's title slink forward, undulating to an insistent rock beat and singing in lemony unison, Bennett was orchestrating the rest of the proceedings—moving a bevy of dancers into the scene, circling the lead girls, prodding them into coolly maintaining their style of movement, urging greater snap and momentum out of everyone else.

As director and cochoreographer (with Michael Peters) of *Dream Girls,* Michael Bennett was the all-pervasive force behind a show that crackles with glitzy glamour and tough emotions: the story of a '60s singing group à la The Supremes that dissects the workings of success, power, fame, failure, love and, above all, relationships both constructive and destructive. Like *A Chorus Line,* it relies on a gutsy score (by Henry Kreiger) and on a bristling, gut-spilling, wisecracking book (by Tom Eyen). But, unlike *A Chorus Line,* its ambience reflects the high-pressure, high-voltage lives of glamorous performers making it in the stratospheric world of superstardom.

"No, it's not the Diana Ross story," Bennett said. "I think Diana will love the show, but it's not about her or The Supremes. The only connection between *Dream Girls* and The Supremes is that they were the most successful of the black-girl singing groups during the '60s, and if they hadn't been so successful, there would never have been a show like *Dream Girls.* So, it's the phenomenon of The Supremes that inspired the show, not the group itself."

Bennett was sitting at his desk in an office the size of a skating rink. No Hollywood mogul ever had it so grand or luxurious. And this was just one of eight floors in the building that he owned on lower Broadway, containing rehearsal halls, offices, conference rooms, and living quarters. Clearly, the place was Bennett's private domain, acquired with the vast income from *A Chorus Line* and renovated not only to house Quadrille (Bennett's corporation), but to be leased out to American Ballet Theatre, the Feld Ballet, and to such theatrical friends as set designer Robin Wagner and costume designer Theoni Aldredge, who have both shops and residences there.

"This building is my hobby," Bennett said. "I've always wanted a home and a place in which to work—and I got it. Eventually, I'm going to build a couple of theaters downstairs on the first floor and maybe a restaurant. It makes it much easier to have everything under one roof. To have Theoni Aldredge and Robin Wagner here makes putting a show together all that much simpler because they are my costume and set designers on *Dream Girls* and their workshops are right here. One doesn't have to race around town for everything.

In a sense, Bennett was talking about control—control over his own life and perhaps the lives of others. And control is also at the heart of *Dream Girls,* which, Bennett says, is not only about the success of a particular singing group, but about the men in their lives—the men who control and manipulate their careers, their marketability, and their business lives.

"I have learned that lesson the hard way, because being a very good business man, which I have had to become, has often conflicted with my being an artist. But, I was willing to take risks, and *Chorus Line* was the perfect example. People forget that I went to work for Joe Papp for $100.00 a week, just so that I could immerse myself in a workshop situation. That's how *Chorus Line* began, and I knew very well that it was a project that wouldn't be of the slightest interest to any commercial producer. It was a cast of dancers who had never even talked on a stage before. It had no stars, no so-called marketability. So, it was taking risks and chances—and it paid off!

"You see, my musicals are very different. They're very tough—very real. They address themselves directly to an audience. They're not elitist in the old-fashioned sense, where one went to the theater and pretended one wasn't there, suspending disbelief. I want an audience to be a part of what I'm saying—my mirrors in *Chorus Line* did that. So, the audience was part of the experience, along with all the associating and relating they did with the characters. Basically, I've tried to change the idea of what a musical is supposed to do. I mean, the form used to be that there's the book, and it takes over for a while, then someone sings a song, then it's time to bring on the dancers. Well, I've mixed up the notion of what the score, the dancing, and what the book are supposed to do. *Chorus Line* was that kind of show, and *Dream Girls* is that kind of show."

There is no question that with the advent of *A Chorus Line* in 1975, Bennett's life changed dramatically. Although he had danced on the Broadway stage and later choreographed and directed a succession of major and minor Broadway productions, notably, *Coco, Company,* and *Follies,* it was *A Chorus Line* that transformed a merely successful artist into what many considered a theatrical genius. Bennett claims that coping with his enormous personal success was something of a trial.

"Talking about success is one of the hardest things in the world ... you have to achieve it to know what it's like. All I can say is that just as a human being, it can get very, very difficult. First of all, so *much* is expected of you! I mean, you couldn't possibly fulfill people's expectations, because the expectations are so unreal. After *Chorus Line* opened, I became a character in the gossip columns, a cartoon character in a comic strip. I read things about myself that had nothing to do with me. I became a public image that was false, and *that* can affect your life. Talk about living in a fishbowl!

"For years, after *Chorus Line,* I tried to balance my success. I'd ask myself, 'Why was I so lucky?' Then came *Ballroom,* my next show, and it was a flop. Well, everybody thought I would be devastated by the failure of *Ballroom*—but I wasn't. I'm still very proud of the show. Yet people thought I'd be destroyed. What everybody seemed to have forgotten was that I had done 15 shows before *Ballroom,* and some of them were big hits and others were flops. So, in a sense, I was prepared for *Ballroom*'s failure. When *Chorus Line* opened and it was a big success, I knew that if I spent the rest of my life chasing the success of *Chorus Line,* I'd be doomed. If I wanted everything to be *more* successful than *Chorus Line,* I'd be working for the wrong reasons. The point is, I don't want to do another *Chorus Line.* When I recently read that *Dream Girls* would be MIchael Bennett's black *Chorus Line,* I thought, 'Oh, no! I'm *not* doing a black *Chorus Line!*'"

If Bennett tried not to let the dazzling success of *A Chorus Line* go to his head, he nevertheless allowed himself to be seduced by at least some of its trappings. For example, he went out and bought himself a Rolls Royce.

"It was the first car I ever owned! I bought it when Donna McKechnie and I got married. Well, I felt so silly in that car, it was ridiculous! You see, when you get very successful, you feel you should get what you want. I always thought Rolls Royces were very beautiful, and I remembered the time when I first came to New York and appeared in my very first musical, *Subways Are for Sleeping.* Well, Betty Comden, who wrote the show with Adolph Green, used to arrive at the theater in a gorgeous Bentley. I used to see it parked outside the theater every day, and I thought, 'When I'm successful, I'm going to have a car like that!' And guess what? When I got successful, I *hated* a car like that! Every pot hole in the city destroyed my Rolls. It was always in the shop being repaired. So, I went on to buy a motorcycle. Then, I went to a Jeep and, later, to a van. Now, finally, I have a regular car ... just a *car* car, like everybody else's."

If *A Chorus Line* boasted a star during its early run, it was undoubt-edly Donna McKechnie, who, like Bennett, had toiled long and hard as a Broadway gypsy and whose subsequent career was closely linked to that of the young and budding dancer, choreographer, and director. In a sense, the off-stage life of McKechnie and Bennett, its joys, complexities, and turmoils, were fully reflected in *A Chorus Line.* With the show's enormous success, they would savor the kind of guileless happiness that comes from life spilling into art and transforming into something tangibly rewarding.

"It was pretty inevitable that Donna and I would get married when *Chorus Line* opened. We both felt that the only person to share all that success with was each other, because it was *our* lives! Well, being married did not work. We were together for about 2 years, and it just didn't work. But that's OK, because I love her *so* much, and we are still friends. It was yet another relationship that should have survived, but didn't. It was what it was. Life changes one, and things have moved very quickly for me. I must say, I'm happier today that I have ever been. I'm not as complicated as I used to be. I go to an analyst, which I've been doing for a number of years, and that's been very, very helpful. I used to scream, 'The world isn't fair!' Then, one day, I woke up and thought, 'Who said it was going to be fair?' So, I'm not as shocked about things as I used to be, and that's easier on my emotions. The fact is, I don't ride up and down emotionally the way I used to."

Bennett smiled wistfully, lit a cigarette, and watched the smoke curling out in front of him.

"You know," he said, "the theater is a funny place to be. It's like a big womb. It represents the perfect world. For me, the strongest frame of reference is being on a stage in a theater. A while back, I went home to Buffalo to visit my mother, and she dragged out my baby pictures and went through my old programs of dance recitals. My very first dance recital was dated June 10, 1945—I was 2-years-old! Can you believe it? And I had started dancing school at 1-1/2! Well, from the very beginning, the theater represented a world where everyone accepted one another, and where everyone loved one another. That's always stuck with me ... this idyllic vision. When I had to face the real world, things became complicated, difficult, mean. I guess that's what *Chorus Line* is all about ... wanting out of the real world and into the perfect world of the theater."

These musings were suddenly interrupted by a call summoning Bennett back into the rehearsal room where *Dream Girls* would continue to be changed, refined, perfected. Bennett got up, put out his cigarette, and slowly walked down a long corridor. Pausing, he said, "You know, I've got a whole new musical planned. It's all in my head, but I won't do it for another 5 or 10 years. It's going to be the story of my life ... the real story, the full story—the works! In the meantime,

I've got to do some more living ... It will be interesting to see where all that living is going to lead me."

Michael Bennett died of AIDS on July 2, 1987. He was 44 years old.

Moira Shearer

Photograph Courtesy of the Dance Collection, The New York Public Library

Moira Shearer

Mention the name Moira Shearer, and movie buffs will instantly smile and say, "Ah, yes! The gorgeous redhead in *The Red Shoes*—the best ballet film ever made!"

But mention *The Red Shoes* to Moira Shearer, and she'll say, "To be constantly associated with that one film is really quite dismaying. It's as though I'd done nothing else in my life. I mean, it's odd, when you're 61, to be haunted by something you had done when you were 21!"

And yet, *The Red Shoes* remains a staple of revival houses the world over, and Ms. Shearer, its star, continues to represent the quintessential young dancer experiencing the agony and ecstasy of being a ballerina. Indeed, more than any ballet movie ever produced (including *The Turning Point, Nijinsky, White Nights,* and *Dancers*), *The Red Shoes* has been the most potently influential dance film ever made.

Completed in England and on location in Monte Carlo in 1947 and released in 1948, this early technicolor film, based on a fairy tale by Hans Christian Andersen, was written and directed by Michael Powell in association with Emeric Pressburger. As a first film of its kind, *The Red Shoes* was given balletic stature and credibility by the presence of Léonide Massine as dancer and Robert Helpmann as choreographer. Shearer was herself a rising young member of London's Sadler's Wells Ballet, which would eventually become the Royal Ballet. The young British actor, Marius Goring, played Shearer's love interest, while the internationally known stage and film star, Anton Walbrook, was cast as the sinister Diaghilev figure, who demands that Shearer choose between a career and love.

If the story of *The Red Shoes* strikes many as being far-fetched and sentimental (the Shearer character kills herself because she *cannot* choose between a career and love), the splendor of the production and the intimate glimpses of backstage ballet life are as vivid and exciting today as they were when the film was first released. Most strikingly, the ballet sequences were staged with remarkable attention to the fluency of the film medium itself. And every glittering, as well as seamy, facet of the ballet world was touched upon with astonishing accuracy. When *The Red Shoes* opened in London and later in New York, it was an instant and lasting success with the public. For Shearer, it was the turning point of her life.

Meeting Shearer in London it seemed as though time had stood still. Ravishingly pretty, her soft red hair still worn as one remembered it in *The Red Shoes,* she offered the image of a dancer's tensile fragility and insouciance. Slim and elegant, the only change was the sound of her voice, no longer that of the tremulous young dancer in the film, but the rich and cultivated voice of an actress, which Shearer became soon after she retired from the ballet stage.

"Please don't make my association with *The Red Shoes* the whole of your article," she pleaded. "That was 40 years ago, and I've done lots of living and working since then."

Indeed, since *The Red Shoes,* Ms. Shearer made five additional films in which she danced and acted with distinction: *The Tales of Hoffman,* again for Powell and Pressburger; *The Story of Three Loves,* an MGM film directed by Sidney Franklin and costarring James Mason and Kirk Douglas; *The Man Who Loved Redheads,* an Alexander Korda film; *Peeping Tom,* which has become something of a cult film from Powell and Pressburger; and *Black Tights,* a ballet film based on works by choreographer Roland Petit.

On the London stage, Shearer appeared as Sally Bowles in John Van Druten's *I am a Camera,* and as Sabina in Thornton Wilder's *The Skin of Our Teeth.* Among other plays, she excelled in Restoration comedies. During the 1970s, she lectured widely on dance throughout Britain and the US. Shearer's first book, *Balletmaster: A Dancer's View of George Balanchine,* was published in America by G.P. Putnam's Sons in 1987. In November, 1987, the BBC aired an hour-long ballet production based on the life of the nineteenth-century British primitive painter, L.S. Lowry. Choreographed by Gillian Lynne of *Cats* and *Phantom of the Opera* fame, the ballet, entitled *A Simple Man* is narrated by Albert Finney and stars the British dancer, Christopher Gable. Shearer dances and mimes the role of Lowry's mother, marking her return to the ballet stage after an absence of some 30 years.

In 1949, Shearer married the noted British journalist and television commentator, Ludovic Kennedy. The couple are the parents of four children, three girls and one boy. There is no question but that Shearer has done a lot of living and working since *The Red Shoes,* even if this singular motion picture has been the vehicle for which she is best remembered. The dancer was willing to recall, as she put it, "the movie I never wanted to make."

"I was happily dancing with the Sadler's Wells Ballet and just beginning to 'come up' with the company," she began. "It was 1946, just after the war, and Margot Fonteyn, our prima ballerina, was dancing in absolutely everything! Of course, she couldn't do every single performance of *Swan Lake* or *Sleeping Beauty,* so some of us got the chance to dance those roles. Well, the film director, Michael Powell, must have come to Covent Garden and seen me in one of those ballets, because I recieved a letter from him asking me to meet him about a film project. We met, and he handed me the script of *The Red Shoes.* He was sure I'd jump at the chance to play the leading girl. I took the script home, read it, and didn't like it at all.

"I told Mr. Powell, as politely as I could, that I didn't want to do this and returned his script. I just thought the story was silly and banal. But he kept insisting. Finally, he went away saying, 'I shall go around the world and find the perfect dancer for this part.' I was delighted. Well, in 1947, Powell was back bombarding me with letters. By this time, Léonide Massine and Robert Helpmann were going to be involved in the movie, and I felt that with those names Powell would at least get the balletic things right. Still, I held out, because I simply didn't like the story.

"But there was no stopping Powell. He badgered and badgered. Finally, Ninette de Valois, our ballet company director, sent for me and said, 'Will you *please* make this movie, and get this man Powell off our backs. He's driving us mad, constantly hanging around the theater and carrying on about you!' I said, 'But what will happen after I finish the movie? Can I come back? Because I want to go on with my ballet career.' She said, 'Absolutely. You can come straight back.' So it was because of that assurance that I agreed to make *The Red Shoes.* It was never because I wanted to do it."

The 6-month filming found Shearer adhering to a grueling dancing and acting schedule. While she found Michael Powell possessed of imagination and originality, she found his working methods almost insupportable. "He had a habit of demolishing people in front of every-one." she said. "It was a dreadful thing to watch." As a novice actress, she felt constrained by her lack of experience and, more importantly, felt that her dancing fell far below her standards—that its technical level seemed insecure and unfocused. Too, she had the gnawing feel-ing that in undertaking this role, British ballet audiences and the ballet world in general would cease to take her seriously as a talented and rising young ballerina. Still, she knew that *The Red Shoes* would be a novel and daring experiment and so did her best to fulfill the rigid demands of the difficult Michael Powell.

"The film was a huge success when it opened at the Plaza Cinema in London in the spring of 1948," Ms. Shearer recalled. "But, just as I had suspected, the British ballet public didn't much approve of my appearing in it. Of course, after the film was completed in 1947, I went straight back to the Sadler's Wells to resume my dancing career, but even there, the reaction was a bit strange. I must say, I never did have an easy time of it in the company, and after the film, it didn't get any easier. I think Ninette de Valois became a bit suspicious of me—she wasn't sure what I might do next. As for me, I was very glad to be back, and I worked as hard as I could to improve as a dancer."

It was in 1948, the year *The Red Shoes* was released, that Shearer achieved a technical breakthrough that would see her performing with new-found brilliance and elan. That year, Frederick Ashton, then the Sadler's Wells's resident choreographer, created Britain's first modern three-act ballet, *Cinderella,* a work meant for Ashton's constant muse, Margot Fonteyn. But Fonteyn suffered a major injury during the early stages of its composition, and the ballet continued to be created upon the specific talents of Shearer. In it, the young dancer scored a personal triumph, and her career began to soar. For the next 4 years, Shearer danced in innumerable works by, among others, Ashton and Massine. Finally in 1952, Balanchine came to London to set his great neoclassic work *Ballet Imperial* (today known as Tschaikowsky Piano Concerto No. 2). The leading part was first danced by Fonteyn, but the ballerina, never a Balanchine fan, soon relinquished this highly complex role, and Shearer once more stepped in, acquitting herself to Balanchine's utmost satisfaction. It was the enthralling experience of working with the choreographer on *Ballet Imperial* that prompted Shearer to writer her memoir on Balanchine, a book that uncharacteristically finds a British dancer extolling an artist whom the British ballet world has never taken to its heart.

Shearer's appearance in Balanchine's *Ballet Imperial* in 1952 would mark the end of her association with the Sadler's Wells Ballet. As time went by she discovered, somewhat to her chagrin, that she had become a star—not for her superb performances in Ashton's *Cinderella* or Balanchine's *Ballet Imperial,* but as the still unformed dancer in *The Red Shoes.*

"The saddest part about it, is that I was not happy with the work I did in that movie, and it's frustrating that people remember me just for *this* out of all the work I ever did," Shearer said. "I just wish I had been a more rounded performer at the time I made it, or that I had done it 2 or 3 years later when I think I could have done justice to it. Still, I've seen *The Red Shoes* a couple of times in the past 10 years, and I must say that for all the creakiness of the dialogue and situations, it has a certain period charm.

"And yes, I must admit, it's given me some good things. For example, would I have gotten a publisher for my Balanchine book so easily if I hadn't been in that film? It's true, *The Red Shoes* has made people remember me, which my ballet and theater career would not have done. So I'm grateful in a sort of backhanded way. I've lived with the spectre of *The Red Shoes* for 40 years. I suppose I'll go on living with it. But isn't it strange that something you've never really wanted to do

turns out to be the very thing that's given you a name and identity?
Ah, well ... life is full of such ironies!"

Peter Martins

George Balanchine and Peter Martins
Photograph by Jack Vartoogian

Peter Martins

With the premiere of his final, three-part version of *Ecstatic Orange,* in June, 1987 at the New York City Ballet, Peter Martins entered the league of major present-day choreographers. The work, set to a propulsive, intensely evocative score by the 25-year-old American composer Michael Torke, and featuring electrifying performances by Heather Watts and Jock Soto, along with stellar soloists and corps, is that rarity: an abstract ballet that fully engages the intelligence and sophistication of an audience by offering clarity of detail within a steely structural whole.

Riding upon Torke's full-blooded, driving sonorities, the ballet is not only a true homage to Balanchine at his most astringent, but at times it moves beyond the master choreographer's inventiveness in matters of complexity and formal variance. We clearly see where this ballet has come from, but also note where Balanchine's great lessons can lead to. It may well be that with *Ecstatic Orange,* Martins has successfully broken the Balanchine barrier.

Certainly in the extended Watts/Soto *pas de deux,* which constitutes the work's second section, Martins has devised a masterful tribute to Balanchine's most astounding eccentricities while retaining his own compelling originality. As for Watts and Soto, who have long been two of Martins's favorite dancers, their singular talents have never been more stunningly put to use. As the company's premiere couple, Watts and Soto here offer artistry of extraordinary brilliance.

Ballet critics have not looked kindly upon the work of Martins. With the notable exception of the *New York Times'* Anna Kisselgoff, the ballet intelligentsia has seen fit to scorn the 30 and more works that Martins has produced since *Calcium Light Night,* created in 1977. Last season, Arlene Croce, dance critic of the *New Yorker,* vented her wrath upon two of Martins's most felicitous works—*Les Petits Riens* and *Les Gentilhommes*—calling the latter a nonballet and merely a "graduation exercise of sorts." As she had done in a previous column, Croce took intense exception to one of *Les Gentilhomme's* dancers, Gen Horiuchi, calling him egregious (meaning "outstanding for undesirable qualities, remarkably bad, or flagrant") and finding his diminutive stature positively offensive.

Martins has become impervious to his critics.

"If these critics were to make a list of 10 world choreographers, they would never include me," he says, "I'm simply not considered a choreographer. Of course, critics are free to say what they want. If

Arlene Croce didn't like *Gentilhommes,* that's her prerogative. But when she starts attacking Gen Horiuchi and does so for the second time, I must object. The fact is, I stopped taking Croce seriously when she attacked him that first time. I thought it was unacceptable. What she fails to note about Horiuchi is his great sense of dignity, something that taller dancers often lack. Anyway, her opinions are quite out of my system, although prior to that first article, I was very interested in her ideas. Now, I've lost interest in her mind."

In his office at the State Theater, where he is Co-Balletmaster-in-Chief of the New York City Ballet, Martins is in an expansive and talkative mood.

"I don't know whether my talent is small or big or medium," he says. "All I know is that I get enormous satisfaction from choreographing. I'm happy making dances, whether it's to Baroque music or to modern music. It may sound strange, but I don't wish to be considered a choreographer with a distinct voice. I have never sought a trademark or a style that would immediately identify me. When I find a piece of music that I adore, I ask myself, 'How can I evoke a feeling about this particular piece of music? How can I make a true visualization of Bach or Mozart or Michael Torke?'

"Obviously, the model is Balanchine. I mean, here was a man who could create *Liebeslieder Walzer* on the one hand, and *Variations pour une porte et un soupir* on the other. Or *The Four Temperaments* one time and *Stars and Stripes* another. And he managed to be right every time. This, to me, is very exciting. You see, I'm not interested in making the same ballet to 17 different scores. Of course, I realize that a style will eventually emerge. I mean, we recognize Balanchine in *Union Jack* just as much as in *Concerto Barocco* and *Who Cares?* The point I'm making is that Balanchine never deliberately set out to work in one recognizable style. A style emerges after a long, long time."

Martins admits that creating for the sake of creating is not his sole motivation. In his position as a company director, he considers it his job to supply dancers with fresh material, with ballets that will hopefully extend their talents and provide them with fresh and stimulating challenges.

In the years since Balanchine's death, Martins and Co-Balletmaster Jerome Robbins have led the New York City Ballet. Martins, in charge of daily operations, is clearly the more active, and his duties are staggering. Although all major decisions are shared with Robbins, Martins hires new dancers from the School of American Ballet (SAB) of which he is chairman of the faculty. He decides which ballets are presented during a given year. He is in charge of casting. He decides who teaches company class and who rehearses what ballets. Often, he teaches class himself. He decides whether the company will tour or not. Within these duties, he must find time to choreograph, which becomes part of the company's complex scheduling apparatus. He attends endless rehearsals and, as balletmaster, coaches many Balanchine ballets. He has made it a policy to keep his door open to dancers wishing to discuss their private or professional problems, a daily occurrence. He lends his presence to fundraising events and engages in fundraising correspondence. What Martins does at the City Ballet is a full-time job in the truest sense of the word.

Martins explains, "We are still a company in transition. And transition can take from 2 weeks to 5 years. It goes without saying that we will always retain the Balanchine repertoire—to what degree remains to be seen. I'm not going to say that next year we'll have 38 percent Balanchine, and the following year, 28 percent Balanchine. I'm going to go with the flow. One of the most important things that has happened is that the Balanchine ballets are now completely on their own. What I mean is, we have lost Balanchine, and because of that, his ballets will remain exactly as he left them. Nobody is allowed to change them. Nobody can alter them for a particular dancer. We've made that a 'law.' You see, Balanchine isn't around to fix up his ballets, which is what he did when he thought they looked old-fashioned. They are now what they are. My view is that they will survive very well.

"As far as dancers are concerned, I'm still going to hire dancers that look best in Balanchine ballets. I happen to like that look in a dancer myself. Where I may differ is in that I like a more individualistic dancer. And yet, Balanchine also liked different kinds of physiques and personalities. Look, it was Balanchine who hired Gen Horiuchi. When he saw Gen in the School of American Ballet Workshop, he turned to me and said, 'Hire him, I want him for *A Midsummer Night's Dream*. I want him to dance Oberon.' So he was hired at Balanchine's command. You see, we have always liked different kinds of dancers, different ways of moving, different approaches to things. Obviously, when you have a corps de ballet, you have to have a certain uniformity. But we are big enough to absorb a few people who are different from the rest.

"But I want to add something else. The world thinks that the New York City Ballet has a particular policy. Well, I can tell you there has never been a policy of any shape or sort or size at the City Ballet. It simply doesn't exist. We go with what is needed at the time. I mean, I was a guest artist for 2 years before joining the company. Mr. B. invited Ghislaine Thesmar from the Paris Opéra Ballet. He invited Jorge Donn from the Béjart company. The fact is, when we need people, we will invite them for a month or a season. There is no fixed policy here."

As a private individual, Peter Martins is without question one of the ballet world's most intriguing men. A public idol as one of the century's greatest and purest classical dancers, this Danish-born artist of Apollonian good looks continues to engage the imagination of many. Although he stopped performing in 1983, his comings and goings continue to be reported in the press. Once briefly married to the Danish dancer Lise La Cour when both were members of the Royal Danish Ballet, Martins is the father of a 20-year-old son, Nilas, currently a corps member of the City Ballet. His long romantic involvement with Heather Watts has been the subject of endless speculation. Choosing to remain single, both have lived together and apart. To this day, Martins's relationship with Watts can only be called profound—a friendship that has endured both turmoil and joy—and which, on a professional level, has brought them both extraordinary fulfillment. And yet, Peter Martins is essentially a man alone.

Martins reflects on his personal life.

"According to the press, my reputation is terrible," he says. "I read the other day that I was a 'walker,' which means I'm somebody who escorts ladies to social events. Without the press, I guess life would be pretty boring! Frankly, I don't have a private life. I only think about things like marriage and having more kids when I'm in my house in Connecticut during the month of August. That's when I become totally domestic. I totally relax. Come 5 o'clock, I break open a bottle of wine, set out some cheese and crackers, and listen to music or watch TV. I prepare dinner. There's a dog running around and a couple of cats in a corner. In the country I come to life. I go out and water the plants. I spray the flowers. A neighbor will walk over and say, 'How are you doing, Pete?' I'm just Pete! And he has no idea who I am or what I do.

"Of course, I think how nice it would be to have a woman there—a wife and maybe a little child. But the problem is, what would they do for the 11 months when I'm at work? Because in New York I leave my apartment at 9:30 in the morning and don't return until 1 or 2 A.M. What would my woman do? And my little child and the little dog and the little cats and the little flowers? Right? So that's the problem. Yes, there's Heather, but she has a big career going. Of course, we see each other a lot, and that's different. Of course, I adore her. Heather is the most generous dancer I've ever known. She is generous in spirit and soul. She is incredibly generous to other dancers. She wishes other people well. Sometimes, it doesn't appear that way, but that's a matter of personality, not character. Heather's character is phenomenal.

"The fact is, Heather, my son—Nilas—and Stanley Williams, who was my teacher from our time together in Denmark, are my three closest friends. With Heather, there have been highs and lows, but we've kept our closeness. Nilas, obviously, is blood. Nilas is on his own now. He's quite independent, which he has always been. He's 20-years-old, and he's leading his own life. We see each other rarely. When we're in the theater, he does his work; I do mine. Sometimes, we have dinner together and chat about things. I see him adjusting to his life. He's only been in this country a couple of years. It's a big change. It took me 5 years to adjust. He's doing very well, and that makes me happy. As for Stanley, who teaches at our school, and whom I hardly ever see or talk to, the bond between us is phenomenal. I may not speak to Stanley for 2 months, and then I'll call him up, and he'll say, 'Hi, sweetheart!' and it's as though we talked only yesterday. I can tell him anything. So, those are my three friends. That's my family.

"Basically, I'm very simple. Absolutely! What pleases me are the simplest things: waking up in the country, having a cup of coffee, standing on my terrace and looking at my view. These things make me happy. What also makes me happy is when the people who are affected by my decisions are happy. When they're happy, I'm happy. It makes me very uncomfortable to see people suffer. I can't bear it whether it's a young dancer suffering because of an injury or not dancing enough or having a bad love affair. Those things make me unhappy."

Martins took another step forward in his growth as Co-Ballet-master of the New York City Ballet in Spring, 1988, when he presented the American Music Festival, a 3-week celebration of American composers to mark the company's 40th anniversary. More than 30 ballets were performed, including world premieres by guest choreographers Jean-Pierre Bonnefoux, Laura Dean, Eliot Feld, William Forsythe, Lar Lubovitch, Paul Taylor, Helgi Tomasson, as well as by company choreographers.

Martins himself was represented by no less than eight world premieres set to such diversified composers as Milton Babbit, John Cage, Philip Glass, Robert Moran, Ellen Zwilich, Michael Torke, Paul Schwartz, Ray Charles, Charles Ives, George Gershwin, Lukas Foss, and Irving Berlin.

Martins saw the festival as an extension of the work of Balanchine. He reacted angrily to those critics who questioned his motivations for staging such am ambitious celebration:

"A lot of people have come to me and said, 'What is this whole American Music Festival about? Why the hell are you inviting all these people who don't know how to choreograph on classical dancers? What are you trying to do?

"Well, maybe by staging this American Music Festival, I'm making a bigger statement. Maybe I'm saying, 'Let's open the gates and let everybody come in and see how things might look.' Don't forget that Balanchine also invited outside choreographers when he staged his festivals. He invited Graham, Cunningham, Tudor, Ashton. It's not unprecedented. I know I'm taking a chance, but I'm convinced the festival will make a statement about our company, about me as a director, and most importantly, about the versatility and talent of all of our dancers. Finally, that's what's important—that's what matters."

In running the New York City Ballet, Martins is aware of the complex feelings his appointment to his post in 1983 has generated. He realizes, with a certain dismay, that there are factions who disapprove of him as a director. In a rare display of candor, Martins talked about this situation.

"Well, I can tell you one thing about the New York City Ballet, and that is that in the immediate future—in 2, 3, maybe 5 years, this company will be up for grabs. The New York City Ballet, which I love, which is my home, and for which I left my country, is up for grabs. I've been running it with Jerry for sometime, but there is a whole world out there that feels I'm not the man for the job—that in one way or another I'm not equipped. There are people out there who feel that somebody else should run this company—and it's from one extreme to the other.

"There are those who think it should be run by Twyla Tharp, who'd come in here and with Jerry Robbins run it and revolutionize it and turn it into what it *ought* to be. Then there are the people who think it should be run by the real heir to George Balanchine: Suzanne Farrell, with or without her husband, Paul Mejia. Then there are those who think that the only true American choreographer today is Paul Taylor—and *he* should be the one. Then, of course, there are those who feel that it should be *just* Jerry Robbins, who is probably the true heir to Balanchine, having spent 45 years in this house. Then there are those who think that the New York City Ballet should simply *die*! So everybody has some idea as to how this place should function.

"So, I'm saying this place is up for grabs. But, who wants it? And who can do it? Don't forget, this is a job where you have to be of service both to the dancers and to the public. Who is going to take care of 105 beautiful dancers coming out of SAB? Who is going to take care of them professionally, feed them new stuff? Who is going to provide them with the material that they require? Because these dancers are highly sophisticated. I know that I have done my utmost for the company. I have not sat on my hands. If I thought I wasn't the right man for the job, I would step down. Absolutely!"